Printed in the United States of America

First Edition
ISBN 0-9631448-9-89
Library of Congress number pending

Virginia Publishing Co.
4814 Washington Blvd., Suite 120
St. Louis, MO 63108
(314) 367-6612

Other books on St. Louis history by Virginia Publishing:
The Days and Nights of the Central West End
St. Louis Lost
The Streets of St. Louis
Lost Caves of St. Louis
Final Resting Place

To Dad, in loving memory.

Acknowledgments

The idea for this book came not from me, but from my dad. He always said that when he retired he was going to write the story of KMOX and talk radio. It would have been a relatively easy project for him since he was involved in the station on a day-to-day basis from almost the beginning of the "At Your Service" days. For me, however, it was a project that started from scratch and enlisted the help of many, many people.

First and foremost, my sincere thanks to CBS and KMOX for the use of all of the material, pictures, and information I found at the radio station. Rod Zimmerman was very supportive of the entire project. Renee LaFlam was always helpful and willing to do whatever she could. Andrew Seigel, from CBS in New York, was always quick to find the answer to my legal concerns.

To my publisher, Jeff Fister, thank you for being as excited about this project as I have been.

To Dr. John Rider and Dr. Jack Shaheen, my former professors at SIUE, your advice, encouragement, and continued friendship over the years have meant so much.

A very special thank-you to Molly Hyland Wight, Bob Hyland's daughter, who allowed me to spend the day in her family room going through her father's notes, tapes, pictures and memorabilia. He was a very special person, Molly.

To Alice Koch English, thank you for the large package of pictures and articles about KMOX and talk radio.

During the months of research, many people were involved with this undertaking. Edward McCarthy, my attorney, was helpful with contracts, releases, and "do's and don't's." Brian Thomas of the Missouri Historical Society spent hours dubbing tapes for me. Charles Brown, from the Mercantile Library, was very helpful in finding every article and picture dealing with KMOX in the *Globe-Democrat* archives. Richard Reilly, from Lovejoy Library at SIUE, assisted me in determining that no book had ever been written about KMOX Radio (much to our amazement).

The personal interviews were so important, and I thank each and every one of you who allowed me time out of your busy schedules — Jim Butler, John Sabin, Bob Costas, Rex Davis, John Angelides, Jack Buck, Bill Wilkerson, Kevin McCarthy, Jeanette Hoag Grider, Anne Keefe, Harvey Voss, Randy Karraker, and Charles Brennan — your information and recollections were invaluable.

To Marita Rinderer and Lucille Chinn, my mother-in-law, thank you for the original recipes you both generously provided. To everyone who sent in a memory or comment, I thank you all.

To Mom, you knew this was something Dad had really wanted to do. You persuaded me to take on this project, and I thank you for the faith you had in knowing I could accomplish it, even though there were times we both thought it would never get done!

And last, but certainly not least, to Glen. Your constant love, and quiet, but ever-present encouragement and support makes every day worth living, and during this project, helped me get through those times when it was just too hard to listen to tapes or the words just didn't come.

Contents

Foreword

What you are about to read (and feel), is the story of an instrument of the highest level for public service. It is also the story of how two men, two Roberts (Hyland and Hardy), came together in history to forge a new concept of radio broadcasting in America. This is a book of "high adventure" on the air waves.

My first experience in radio came when I was about nine or ten years of age, when my father, who was one of the first very successful merchants to see the vision of what broadcasting could be, took me over a bumpy dirt road in the early evening, into the countryside around Westfield, Illinois, to deliver a "wet" (B) battery to a country home. As we neared the home, I could see the Aladdin lamp sending flickering shadows across the faces of people, sitting with great expectancy in a circle in front of a silent radio set. When my father attached the battery, it was as if a giant light bulb (no electricity yet) had been switched on. Faces lit up, people leaned forward as the sound of Grand Ole Opry came from the speaker.

I came of age along with the development of radio, and spent most of my professional life as reporter, announcer and then teacher in the field. I was a part of the development of this medium as it came to grips with the challenges of the times.

During the "golden years" of radio, when Ma Perkins, Mr.

Keene, the Lone Ranger, Fibber McGee and Molly, and a host of others dominated one's evening hours, there began a quiet development of radio as the primary source of breaking news, information and commentary for public consumption. When that crest broke on the shores of a maturing republic, two men, Bob Hyland, who often had a solitary vision of what public service could and should be, and Bob Hardy, who became one of the most trusted reporters of our time, came together in time to create the premier programming concept which, although has recently suffered some amelioration of its noblest ideals, still continues as the example of the basic purpose of the medium.

Over the years I have found great pleasure in creating and directing the Department of Mass Communications at Southern Illinois University. One of our principal supporters, and often mentor, was Bob Hardy. We talked on the phone regularly about things in the medium, he received our students as observers and was always willing to come across the river to talk with students and faculty alike when asked, and he (and Re) had the wisdom to send Sandy to us for her media education.

When we first moved to Edwardsville, in the summer of 1968, I turned on the radio on that first morning and heard those well-rounded tones.... "This is Bob Hardy ... on KMOX, St. Louis." There was never a morning, until very recently, when that was not the introduction to the days of my life.

I miss him ... his objectivity, his dedication to truth, his commitment to fairness, his repertorial skills, but mostly for his friendship. Open the book, dear reader, and reap a bountiful harvest of hope and remembrance.

John R. Rider, Ph.D.
Professor Emeritus
Southern Illinois University at Edwardsville

KMOX Firsts

- The inauguration in 1960 of "At Your Service," the trend-setting, community-oriented information format now known as "talk radio" in the broadcasting industry;
- The first CBS-owned radio or television station to editorialize;
- The first CBS-owned radio or television station to endorse a political candidate (June 23, 1958);
- The first station in the nation to use the Conelrad warning system for severe weather conditions (later adapted nationally by the United States Weather Bureau);
- The first station to broadcast during sessions from both houses of the Missouri legislature;
- The first station to schedule a member of the Foreign Diplomatic Corps as an entertainment personality (James Duffy, British Consul in St. Louis);
- The first commercial radio station to broadcast complete baseball games from outside the continental United States (the Cardinals trip to Japan in 1958);
- The first radio station to broadcast National League Football live from overseas (the Big Red vs. the San Diego Chargers from Japan in August 1976);
- The first commercial radio station in the nation to broadcast a college credit course;
- The first station to broadcast an open-heart surgery;

• The first station locally to use leading civic leaders as substitute personalities, allowing them the use of air-time to describe their favorite cause;

• The first station to form a liaison with the St. Louis Police Department to help drivers avoid hazardous situations on regional highways;

• The first CBS-owned station to have a woman station manager — Virginia Dawes;

• One of the first radio stations to establish Call for Action, a volunteer service program offering needed assistance to people, by referring them to the appropriate community resources;

• One of the first radio stations to appoint an ecology editor;

• Had one of its own, Bob Hardy, as one of eleven U.S. journalists to accompany eight governors to the Soviet Union (October 1971);

• Originated a "radio bridge," a monthly satellite link between KMOX and Moscow Radio, hosted by Bob Hardy (December 1989);

• Sponsored a trip, setting new standards for the industry, with Bob Hardy broadcasting live from five Eastern European capitals. The five, one-hour long "At Your Service" programs culminated with the first live broadcast back to the United States from Red Square in Moscow (April 1990).

• KMOX Radio was the only station to win all three major Marconi awards:

1991 — Legendary station of the year;

1990 — Major market station of the year;

1989 — News-talk station of the year.

Introduction

KMOX Radio was not the first radio station in the country. It was not even the first radio station in St. Louis. But that is where not being first ends, because KMOX became the radio station that everyone, not just in the United States, but all over the world, wanted to copy. KMOX was like a beacon in the night for which others in the industry reached. The "jewel in the CBS crown," a nickname given to the station by CBS founder William Paley, was the pinnacle by which other stations measured their success.

And while other stations were copying "The Voice of St. Louis," KMOX was moving forward, making its mark in, and on, the community it served. "When the full legendary staff was in place in the '60s and '70s — there may never have been a radio station anywhere that had that kind of stable of talent, that had that kind of impact on its community, not just in ratings which you can measure, but in the way in which intangibly it seemed to become part of the fabric of the community and the official voice of the community,"[1] says Bob Costas, who got his start at the station. KMOX had an overwhelming power over the community. It was more than a radio station; it was the authority — on everything!

From its inception, community was what KMOX was all about. Members of the community trusted and relied on KMOX, and the station's family became a part of every family who had their radio tuned to 1120. When KMOX lost a member of its family, the whole community grieved because of that sense of kinship.

KMOX, "The Voice of St. Louis," was the station's name from the beginning. But who *was* "the voice" of KMOX? It was Bob Hardy, a man who for thirty-three years the listening audience called "Mr. Radio News." Hardy received honors and awards from more than fifty media, civic and service organizations, and was admired by thousands, both professionally and personally, for his integrity, dignity, truthfulness, and humility.

Expressing her memories of Hardy in 1993, Lucy Ann Boston, "Life Style" reporter and former *St. Louis Globe-Democrat* reporter said, "To Bob, the story was the star, he wasn't the star ... he never considered himself a celebrity ... the people he covered was the most important thing.... He was an incredible pro and ... [someone] for all of us to emulate in the rest of our careers."[2]

A KMOX listener said of Hardy, "He was a champion of the listener ... he made us the best listeners in the world."[3] Hardy realized that his audience trusted him; a responsibility he did not take lightly. Remembering Hardy, Charles Osgood said, "What radio does at its very, very best is to keep you company as if you were there with a friend, and [Bob] was really just like that for, I'm sure, thousands and thousands of people."[4]

The St. Louis community loved Bob Hardy, a love reciprocated by Hardy for his adopted hometown. Says close friend, Colonel Leonard Griggs, "He gave so much to St. Louis and all who knew him."[5] It was important to Hardy, being able to give back to a community that had given him so much.

Once Hardy joined the KMOX family, he never considered another professional move. "KMOX was right where he wanted to be ... he was happy and secure [where he was],"[6] says Costas.

KMOX and Bob Hardy were a perfect match. The "Voices" of St. Louis grew together, carving out a niche in St. Louis broadcasting history that may never be equaled.

A New Station

On December 24, 1925, KMOX, the new super station known as "The Voice of St. Louis" took to the airwaves and was hailed as a "gift to America."[7]

Earlier that year, a group of St. Louis businesses had formed The Voice of St. Louis, Inc., a Missouri corporation organized with the intention of owning and operating a radio station that represented the various business and civic interests of the state. The station's purpose was not only educational and cultural, but also to bring St. Louis to the attention of a larger audience, and thereby increase the number of businesses and visitors to the city. As J. Sheppard Smith, president of the Mississippi Valley Trust Company, explained to the *Globe-Democrat* on December 19, 1925, "We realize that radio is not only the greatest scientific wonder of the age, but also promises to become the greatest educational and cultural influence of centuries.... Aside from its educational and cultural aspects, radio has a place in commerce.... Since radio broadcasting has no means of collecting a fee from the beneficiaries of the great service it renders, it devolves upon public-spirited individuals and institutions to contribute to its upkeep. [We are glad] to help give St. Louis and the nation a great super-power station that will not only entertain millions of families, but educate them and make their minds turn to the great city the station represents.... Those who are fortunate enough to reside in this great industrial center, surrounded as it is by the entire United States, will be brought to a greater appreciation of their home city…. Those who live from ocean to ocean will become better acquainted with the industrial advantages and splendid living conditions of St. Louis, and this is bound to bring new industries and new people into our midst."[8]

The original members of The Voice of St. Louis, Inc. were Wagner Electric Co., the St. Louis Radio Trades Association, the *St. Louis Globe-Democrat*, the St. Louis Southwestern Railway, Skouras Brothers Theatrical Enterprises, Merchants Exchange, the Mayfair Hotel and, the Mississippi Valley Trust Company. By the time the station went on the air, the corporation also included the Blanke Tea and Coffee Co., the Blanke Candy Co., Brown Shoe Co., E. Davis Realty Mortgage Co., the Kennedy Corporation, George Kilgen & Son, Stark Brothers Nurseries and Orchards Co., and F.C. Taylor Fur Company.

In December 1925, the Department of Commerce assigned "The Voice of St. Louis" its call letters, KMOX. In October of that year, the new station had tentatively been assigned the call letters "KVSL," in keeping with the name of the station. But the St. Louis corporation wanted a three-letter call sign and requested "KMO." These letters were already assigned to a small station on the West Coast, so the addition of the letter "X" was agreed upon.

Since the beginning, the meaning of the call letters has been up for debate. This stems from a comment by then mayor of Kirkwood, R. L. Jacobsmeyer. Kirkwood was where the transmitter for the super station was located. The ground for the transmitting station was donated by Kirkwood Trust Company and when the call letters were assigned, Jacobsmeyer said KMOX means, "Kirkwood, Missouri's Xmas Gift to the World."[9]

Jacobsmeyer was on the right track, but in all actuality, the call letters stand for: K, indicating the government designation for a radio station west of the Mississippi River; MO for Missouri; and X for Christmas.

One week before the formal opening of KMOX, the station tested its broadcast capabilities. The result was a deluge of

KNOW ALL MEN BY THESE PRESENTS: That we, the undersigned, desirous of forming a corporation under the laws of Missouri, and more particularly under the provisions of Article
VII, Chapter 90, Revised Statutes of Missouri, 1919, and amendments thereto, covering
manufacturing and business companies, have entered into the following agreement:

First: The name of the corporation shall be VOICE OF ST. LOUIS, INCORPORATED.

Second: The corporation shall be located in the City of St. Louis, Missouri.

Third: (a) The total number of shares authorized is seven hundred and fifty (750)
shares, which shares are without nominal or par value.
(b) The amount of capital with which the corporation will begin business is
Twenty-five Thousand Dollars ($25,000.00), which is paid up in lawful money of the United
States and is in the custody of the persons named as the first Board of Directors or
Managers.

Fourth: The names and places of residence of the shareholders and the number of
shares subscribed by each are as follows:

Name	Residence	No. of Shares
Frank H. Sullivan	St. Louis, Missouri	100
Edward W. Lake	St. Louis, Missouri	100
Frank A. Mohr	St. Louis, Missouri	100
Arthur W. Schmoeller	St. Louis, Missouri	100
Warren P. Drescher, Jr.	St. Louis, Missouri	100

Fifth: The Board of Directors shall consist of five (5) shareholders, and the following
named shareholders have been agreed upon for the first year, to-wit:
Frank H. Sullivan
Edward W. Lake
Frank A. Mohr
Arthur W. Schmoeller
Warren P. Drescher, Jr.

Sixth: The corporation shall continue for a term of fifty (50) years.

Seventh: The corporation is formed for the following purposes, to-wit: to contract, own
and operate a radio telephone broadcasting station, and to arrange for the giving of concerts, lectures, musical and other entertainments, and for the broadcasting of same, and
to this end to employ singers, musicians, lecturers, speakers, and other entertainers; and for
the broadcasting of concerts, lectures and entertainments given by others; also for the
broadcasting of news, market reports, stock, security, grain and produce quotations, and
other information usually given by means of the stock ticker and other tape tickers; and
to do all things that may be properly done incidental to the foregoing purposes, and to have
all the rights and privileges in this State and in the United States and in foreign countries
which accrue to manufacturing and business corporations under the laws of the State of Missouri.

In Witness Whereof, we have hereunto set our hands this 30th day of September, 1925.
Frank H. Sullivan
Edward W. Lake
Frank A. Mohr
Arthur W. Schmoeller
Warren P. Drescher, Jr.

State of Missouri),
City of St. Louis)ss

On this 30th day of September, 1925, before me personally appeared Frank H. Sullivan,
Edward W. Lake, Frank A. Mohr, Arthur W. Schmoeller and Warren P. Drescher, Jr., to me known
to be the persons described in and who executed the foregoing instrument and acknowledged
that they executed the same as their free act and deed.

In Testimony Whereof, I have hereunto set my hand and affixed my Notarial seal, the day
and year last above mentioned.

My commission expires Oct. 12, 1927

Emilee H. Blird
Notary Public

COPY OF SEAL
Emilee H. Blird
Notary Public
City of St. Louis, Mo.

Filed & Recorded October 30th, 1925 at 10:32 A.M.

Wm. L. Thoma, Recorder.

The original articles of incorporation. *KMOX Radio*

congratulatory telegrams and long-distance telephone calls from such cities as Vancouver, Washington; Baltimore, Maryland; and San Mateo and San Diego, California. A radio enthusiast in Colorado, who had picked up the trial broadcast, placed a phone call to Managing Director Thomas Convey and proved the great reception by placing his receiver against the telephone mouthpiece. Western Electric engineers monitored the broadcast in this way for two minutes, and were surprised at the quality.

Inspections at the station and transmitter were completed early, which allowed for the broadcast test to start unexpectedly. At the start of the broadcast, Convey informed the audience that announcer Nate Caldwell was absent because the tests had not been scheduled for this time. Caldwell, who had only arrived in St. Louis days earlier, had been the chief announcer at WBBM in Chicago. He and

A Steinway concert grand piano and a Kilgen organ, located in one of two studios at the Mayfair Hotel, when KMOX first went on the air in 1925. *St. Louis Mercantile Library Association*

a friend were tuning up different radio stations that evening and heard Convey's announcement about his absence. Caldwell got into a "high power automobile, stepped on the gas and onto Manchester Road, through the Brentwood speed trap ... and was at the micro-phone in less than fifteen minutes after he heard the apology."[10]

Christmas Eve, 1925, was the day the investors and the audience had waited for. KMOX went on the air from its new studios, located in the Mayfair Hotel, with a power of 5,000 watts on a frequency of 1,070 kc. The studios were elaborate by any standards. The reception room included tapestry wall hangings and subdued lighting to remind guests of a club-type atmosphere. Both studios were decorated with wall hangings of a burnt-amber color and gathered to a ceiling sunburst effect, complete with fabric rosettes in the center. French satin brocade drapes covered the upper portions of the doors. Portable platforms would be available whenever a large musical group performed at the station. Each studio contained a Steinway concert grand piano, and a Kilgen organ was located behind a decorative grill leading into the main studio. Visitors to the studios were separated from the artists by double glass-insulated partitions.

The inaugural program on Christmas Eve began with ad-dresses from those who had brought the new station to frui-tion. Christmas music was performed by the St. Peter's Epis-copal Church choir. The first official message of KMOX came from announcer Nate Caldwell, and was followed by a short organ selection. Then the Little Symphony orchestra per-formed "The Star-Spangled Banner," and "Hail To The Chief."

In his address that night, the mayor of St. Louis stressed the importance KMOX would play in teaching people around the country about the industrial, educational, religious and com-munity development of the city. He spoke of civic service and the duty of the community in the building and advancement of a city. "Those who are responsible for this great broadcast-ing station are keeping step with the new spirit of St. Louis.... It is through this agency that the spirit of St. Louis will spread throughout the country and will result in the mutual benefit of all."[11]

E. Lansing Ray, president and editor of the *St. Louis Globe-Democrat* and chairman of the board of directors of "The Voice of St. Louis," spoke of the importance of KMOX in bringing the entertainments of the city — music, lecture and drama — as well as scientific discoveries and information for the men of industry and commerce[12] to those who lived far from the city center.

Clarence Howard, president of Commonwealth Steel Company, officially accepted KMOX on behalf of its millions of unseen listeners. Howard spoke of how the station could tell those listeners about St. Louis as being centrally located — geographically, industrially, and in its population. "To our listeners in the East, we say that St. Louis embodies your Eastern culture; to the North we say we have your energy plus the hospitality of the South and the vision of the West … and while our industries are shipping from the center and not the rim, our station KMOX is radiating from the center to the rim of our country, the Golden Rule fellowship spirit of St. Louis."[13]

And radiating it was. On January 17, 1926, the St. Louis Globe-Democrat *published a letter sent to KMOX from George Munro of University College in Auckland, New Zealand. Over 8,000 miles away, Munro spoke of the remarkable clarity and unusually clear reception during the station's first official on-the-air tests on December 16.[14] In addition, during the first weeks KMOX was on the air, letters came from Hawaii, Alaska, Mexico, and every state in the nation.*

Station owners around the country realized their stations must broadcast the highest-quality programs available, and the Voice of St. Louis, Inc., was no different. Sponsorship of programs on the new station allowed the members of the corporation to receive the publicity that went along with sponsorship.

Programming during KMOX's first months on the air was as diverse as the businesses that owned the station. Market reports were heard daily, sponsored by the Merchants Exchange. The Radio Trades Association presented an afternoon musical hour. Geared towards women, C.F. Blanke Tea and Coffee Co. and C.F. Blanke Candy Co. offered a daily hour-long program devoted to providing information on problems unique to the housewife and the care of a household. George Kilgen & Son, Inc., sponsored Arthur Utt presiding at the in-studio organ. *Associated Press* news reports were broadcast nightly by the *St. Louis Globe-Democrat.* Buster Brown featured a variety of entertainment for children and adults. Stark Brothers Nurseries sponsored a program that was reminiscent of the little red schoolhouse — there was a five-minute segment on the gardening topic of the day, a five-minute "recess," and then a five-minute segment on another gardening

Gene Rodemich's jazz orchestra. *St. Louis Mercantile Library Association*

topic. The Cotton Belt Hour featured civic and musical organizations from other cities. The ten-piece Little Symphony orchestra, under the direction of David Bittner Jr., as well as a twelve-piece jazz orchestra under the direction of Gene Rodemich, were heard regularly and sponsored at different times by the F.C. Taylor Fur Co., Wagner Electric Co., the Davis Realty and Mortgage Co., the Mayfair Hotel, and the Colin B. Kennedy Corporation.

From the January 4, 1926, *St. Louis Globe-Democrat*, listed under Radio by the Clock —

Today's Program from Station KMOX
9:30 a.m. to 1 p.m. — At thirty-minute intervals, market reports direct from the floor of the Merchants Exchange, closing reports at 1 p.m. following organ recital.

Noon to 1 p.m. — Organ recital by Arthur L. Utt, on Kilgen studio organ.

3 to 5 p.m. — Benny Washington and his Six Aces, with soloists in mixed program.

7 to 8 p.m. — Mixed program; Miss Ruth Hartmiller, soprano, and other soloists.

8 to 10 p.m. — Little Symphony orchestra, conducted by David L. Bittner Jr.; soloists: Jules Waldock, tenor; half hour with Rudyard Kipling, readings by staff reader; songs by Chester Merton, tenor.

10 to 10:30 p.m. — Mixed program.

10:30 to 11:30 p.m. — Dance music by Gene Rodemich and his orchestra.

11:30 p.m. to Midnight — Arthur L. Utt, on studio Kilgen organ.

Midnight to 1 a.m. — Gene Rodemich and his twenty-eight piece orchestra.[15]

In addition to regular programming, the broadcast day also included unscheduled time, which was available to people who wanted to come on the air and present what was referred to as "courtesy programs." This allowed the station to fill its broadcast day without having to pay the person who was on the air. Elizabeth Cueny, who headed up the musical staff, was in charge of selecting guests for these hours, and the station was very particular about what would go on the air. Cueny said, "From the many applications received for the broadcast privilege, only the best will be chosen."[16]

The Early Years

Three months after the station went on the air, a group organized for the purpose of monitoring the station, selected KMOX as being the best they had ever heard on radio.

It was at this same time that George Junkin arrived at KMOX from WSWS in Chicago to take the position of chief announcer. Junkin, who by year's end would be the station's managing director, praised the station upon his arrival. "I consider KMOX one of the five leading broadcasters in America. Its financial condition, its management, personnel, equipment, facilities, and program material, place it easily within this group … and I am glad to join the staff of KMOX for this reason."[17]

There were many highlights during that first year on the air. On April 30, 1926, KMOX broadcast Sir Thomas Malory's *Morte d'Arthur*, the first of its Tabloid Novel Series. The idea of the series was to broadcast a famous novel in a ten-minute condensed version. The concept, successfully used on the lecture circuit in England, had not yet been adapted to radio until KMOX gave it a try. Edgar Curtis Taylor, a Washington University English instructor, was given the task of condensing and broadcasting twelve outstanding novels. The series was a smashing success.

Baseball was also featured, with the Cardinals winning the 1926 World Series.

KMOX made arrangements with the *Associated Press* to

broadcast the returns of the August primary elections as they were received by the *St. Louis Globe-Democrat*.

In cooperation with the St. Louis Safety Council, KMOX instituted the Careful Children's Club for the purpose of

The cover page from a 1928 radio log, featuring KMOX personalities.
KMOX

training children in safety habits. By December 1926, over 25,000 school children in the St. Louis area listened to Safety Sam and the Careful Twins talk about the dangers of playing in the streets, hitching rides on vehicles, the hazards of dangling wires, and much more.

As the holiday season and KMOX's first anniversary approached, "The Voice of St. Louis" asked its thousands of listeners to help make the holidays happy for the poor and needy children of the city. The request resulted in close to 125,000 donations.

It was a year of change and continued success for KMOX in 1927. In June, the frequency was changed from the original 1,070 kc to 1,000 kc., but for the time being, the power remained at 5,000 watts.

In September, KMOX, "The Voice of St. Louis," became one of the original stations under an oral agreement with the United Independent Broadcasters, which eventually became CBS. CBS agreed to provide telephone circuits and to pay $500 a week for ten hours of broadcast time. The first CBS broadcast in St. Louis was on September 18, 1927, and the ten CBS hours per week were heard on Mondays, Wednesdays and Fridays from 9 until 11 p.m., and on Sundays from 3 to 5 p.m. and 9 till 11 p.m. In December, KMOX became a charter CBS Radio Network affiliate.

The highlight of the 1927 broadcast year for KMOX was welcoming Charles Lindbergh home to St. Louis after his triumphant solo flight to Paris in "the Spirit of St. Louis."

REPEATING RIFLE
Given Away Each Day
To Some One of Our
RADIO LISTENERS
During the Taylor program which is broadcast every morning except Sunday, between 6:45 and 7:00 a.m. from Radio Station KMOX, Uncle Lem will mention the name and address of some man or boy whose name is upon the Taylor mailing list. If the person whose name is mentioned will write to Uncle Lem care Radio Station KMOX, St. Louis, Mo., we will send him absolutely free a high grade .22 caliber repeating rifle. Listen each morning for the name selected may be your own.

A promotion sponsored by the F.C. Taylor Fur Co. and KMOX in 1928. This announcement was included in a newspaper ad. *KMOX*

In September, the value of KMOX and its broadcast capabilities was evident after a destructive tornado swept through the city. Over half of the members of the St. Louis Naval Reserve unit responded to an on-the-air plea for assistance. Within 48 hours, over $20,000 had been raised for the victims.

Another broadcast of 1927 brought tears to listeners when, in July, KMOX helped reunite an orphaned brother and sister after twenty-one years.

Ada Wallace of Mount Vernon, Illinois, had been trying to locate her younger brother, Charles, for years. After receiving information with her brother's adopted name, Clavin, she continued her search, but was unsuccessful. Her cousin suggested a broadcast on KMOX. After getting permission from the police, she made a three-minute announcement on "The Voice of St. Louis." One week later, the two siblings met, seeing each other for the first time since she was eight and he was five months old.

Sports got a new voice in 1927 with the arrival of Bill Mack, founder of the "Hot Stove League." Mack split his time between the training camps of the St. Louis Browns and Cardinals, and sent detailed reports back to St. Louis for broadcast each evening. Mack was the sports voice of KMOX until 1930, when he was replaced by France Laux, who was voted the top sports announcer in St. Louis in a contest sponsored by the *Globe-Democrat*.

There always seemed to be something special and exciting happening on KMOX. At 6 p.m. on April 20, 1928, listeners heard Big Ben, the clock on the House of Parliament in London, chime midnight. William West, an engineer at KMOX, had been working out of his home trying to pick up station 5FW out of Chelmsford, England. Just before hearing Big Ben, KMOX listeners were enjoying orchestral music from the Terrace Garden in London.

In June, proceedings of the Kansas City political convention were broadcast.

November 1928 signaled another frequency change for "The Voice of St. Louis," as well as good news about its future. The Federal Radio Commission assigned 1,090 kc exclu-

Charley Stookey in 1932. *Alice Koch English*

sively to KMOX, and gave the station the go-ahead to begin construction on a new 50,000-watt tower. The site for the new structure was located on twenty-five acres, just east of Clarkson Road. The location was considered perfect because it was more than twenty-five miles due west of the city, with the nearest town being Ellisville.

On the new frequency in September 1929, the station began broadcasting with a power of 50,000 watts. This put KMOX, "The Voice of St. Louis," in a very select group, with just a handful of other members.

As the new decade began, the contract that brought the CBS network and KMOX together was being modified. The new contract would change the dollar amount that CBS paid the station for broadcast rights of commercial programs as well as cancel the limited hours for these broadcasts. Additionally, the

The 1933 KMOX staff. *St. Louis Mercantile Library Association*

network would offer other programs for broadcast, without cost to the station, and allow the station to sell time during these broadcasts to local advertisers.

During this period, CBS began a two-and-a-half-year process of buying out the owners of The Voice of St. Louis, Inc. In September 1932, CBS was the sole owner of 2,563 shares of capital stock for which they had paid $339,200, making KMOX a CBS-owned and -operated station. By year's end, the network's "O & O's" included: WABC, New York; WBBM, Chicago; WBT, Charlotte; WCCO, Minneapolis; WJSV, Washington; WKRC, Cincinnati; WPG, Atlantic City; and KMOX.

The purchase was made final four years later, when on December 5, 1936, The Voice of St. Louis, Inc., assigned its license for KMOX to CBS.

The 1930s also found KMOX embroiled in a lawsuit with another area radio station, KWK. In a $100,000 damage suit, radio station KWK sued KMOX over an alleged effort to prevent a KWK broadcast of the landing of the St. Louis *Robin*, which had made a record endurance flight the previous summer. The two stations settled out of court. There was no cash involved in the settlement,

KMOX personalities Henry, Zeb and Otto, featured on the station in the late '20s and early '30s. *KMOX*

but rather, an agreement was reached concerning the next season's baseball games whereby both stations would have equal privileges.

The station continued to log "firsts." The world first heard about the spring flooding, and the devastation it caused along the Mississippi River, from KMOX. Listeners were amazed when they heard KMOX's first-ever radio broadcast of a conversation between the occupants of an airplane in flight and its ground station. KMOX worked in cooperation with Universal Divisions of American Airways and the government airways radio station at Lambert Field to bring the first-of-its-kind broadcast to listeners.

A mythical character, known as the "Spirit of St. Louis," became a weekly visitor for KMOX listeners. Every Sunday, during the intermissions of the St. Louis Symphony Orchestra broadcasts, the "Spirit" would introduce new places of interest, relate exciting happenings, and extol the virtues and highlights of the city.

Conducting a trip to many lands, the mythical "Spirit of St. Louis," took his radio audience on a tour of St. Louis foreign quarters…. "Only a few of the thousands who daily travel the main roads of St. Louis are aware of the beauty and Old-World charm of the scores of quaint bi-paths that wind through this metropolis of many lands. Founded as a French settlement, the population of St. Louis later became predominantly German, and today many [other] nationalities are represented in this city."[18]

In an effort to find and develop local talent, "The Voice of St. Louis" announced the opening of a training school for musical and dramatic artists. The new Artists Bureau and Radio Training School worked in conjunction with music schools, organizations and artists throughout the city, and was the first organization of its kind in the Midwest. Just two months after opening, more than fifty musicians, singers, and other artists were affiliated with the Bureau, and KMOX contracted with them to furnish talent for its radio programs.

Early in 1932, the studios and offices moved to the new $5 million St. Louis Mart Building located at the corner of

Twelfth Boulevard and Spruce Street. The new complex occupied two floors of the Mart Building, and was three times larger than the original studios at the Mayfair Hotel.

A significant feature of the new facility, including six studios, was that all of the studios were suspended by steel springs, allowing them to "float." This concept, used with soundproofing materials, prevented vibrations and sound in one studio from bleeding through to another studio. In addition, the ceilings were adjustable and could be raised or lowered to attain the best acoustical effects for broadcasts.

CBS praised the new facilities and equipment as being the most efficient and modern in the country, and announced plans to use KMOX as the originating station for many of the CBS programs broadcast throughout its system. This would mean many successful radio artists and entertainers would be

Merle Jones, general manager (left), and Francis Douglas, news director, in 1942. *St. Louis Mercantile Library Association*

visiting the KMOX studios.

But "The Voice of St. Louis" was serving more than just the St. Louis area. KMOX was selected by the Royal Canadian Mounted Police to broadcast a message several times a week to isolated detachments in the northernmost part of Canada. It was determined that KMOX was well received in northern Canada, and the broadcasts would continue indefinitely until the service was no longer needed by the Mounties.

J.L. Van Volkenburg was named the new president of the station in June 1933. Van Volkenburg, who at twenty-nine became the youngest head of any major broadcasting station in the country, had previously held the positions of sales manager and director of operations at KMOX.

Contests and give-aways were always a draw for listeners. In 1933, KMOX used singer Bing Crosby's popularity as the basis for a radio contest. In July, KMOX and the Ambassador Theater co-sponsored a contest to find a young man in St. Louis who sounded the most like the famous crooner. There were 250 contestants, and the winner was 21-year-old Eddie Wacker Jr. of South Kingshighway. His prize was a one-week engagement at the theater.

Roy Queen had the first country band to feed the network from St. Louis in 1931. He was part of the KMOX family through the 1950s. *KMOX*

By September 1938, KMOX was the largest radio station in St. Louis, with 120 employees (compared with 20 employees 10 years earlier), and paying approximately $400,000 annually in salaries.

In 1941, KMOX was assigned a new frequency of 1120 on the radio dial during a national reallocation of wavelengths, a frequency that remains to this day. The station also became one of twenty-four clear channel stations in the United States, meaning the dial frequency 1120 was, and would continue to be, exclusively assigned to KMOX.

During the 1940s, the station continued its innovative approach with live, variety talent programs featuring both amateurs and professionals from the Midwest. One such program was "Saturday at the Chase," a broadcast of whoever was performing that particular night at the Chase Park-Plaza Hotel. These programs were picked up by the CBS network, and sent to all of its affiliates. Usually the talent was not quite "big-name" yet, but the national radio exposure certainly helped many careers. Among those appearing on KMOX were Marvin Miller, who later appeared in television's "The Millionaire," and George Gobel, who went on to have his own comedy series on the CBS Television Network.

In the late '40s, Harry Fender hosted a two-hour record show each weekday afternoon from his apartment.

Harvey Voss, who was with KMOX from 1939 until 1978, recalls the afternoon programs. In addition to Fender, "There were three of us at his apartment — a producer, an engineer, and a 'platter man.' It was a union thing, and we had to have a musician handle and cue any record we played on the air."[19]

Live studio audiences were an important part of the entertainment programs of the '40s, and the studios in the Mart Building were often full. "Uncle Dick Slack's Barn Dance," featuring Pappy Cheshire and his Hillbillies, was such a popular Saturday night program that guests often had to wait up to six weeks for tickets.

"Summer in St. Louis" was a long-running weekly program in the late '40s and early '50s. The show coincided with the Municipal Opera season, and provided good publicity for the Muny, as the show was carried over the entire CBS network. Originating from the station's studios and using the staff band, a featured singer from the week's performance at the Muny would present a program of the show's music. The program was very popular, and eagerly awaited by the listening audience each summer.

The station added to its trophy case in March of 1947 when it was awarded a citation by the National Conference of Christians and Jews for its historical program, "The Land We Live In." The tribute named KMOX as the station in the United States which had made the greatest contribution to furthering understanding and goodwill in 1946.

KMOX was one of only fifteen radio stations in the country with 50,000 watts of power, and on the evening of April 8, 1947, a new 50,000-watt transmitter was dedicated during special programming. The new tower, which replaced the one used for the past ten years in St. Louis County, was located approximately eleven miles away in Stallings, Illinois. The new transmitter improved the quality of reception, reached an estimated 25 percent more homes, covered a 39 percent larger territory, and used 25 percent less power.

The popularity of KMOX and its programs was evident in February 1949, when the station was off the air for an hour and twenty minutes due to a cable break at the transmitter site.

Telephone switchboards at KMOX, the St. Louis Globe-Democrat *and police headquarters were jammed by thousands of callers when a broken cable caused listeners to miss the entire "Jack Benny Program" and the "Amos 'n Andy Show," the last ten minutes of "The Spike Jones Show," and the first ten minutes of "The Adventures of Sam Spade." According to Wendall Campbell, KMOX's general manager, "It couldn't have happened at a worse time — Benny's show is one of the more popular on the air."*[20]

The incident, though unfortunate, proved that "The Voice of St. Louis" had an enormous audience.

KMOX's Visionary

The early '50s saw many changes in management at KMOX. In August 1951, Robert F. Hyland Jr. returned to his hometown of St. Louis to become national sales manager for KMOX.

Hyland grew up on Lindell Boulevard, and attended Barat Hall and Saint Louis University High School. He was the son of Dr. Robert F. Hyland Sr. and Genevieve Burks Hyland. Known as "the surgeon of baseball," the senior Hyland was the team physician for the St. Louis Cardinals and the St. Louis Browns. Through his father, Hyland met many sports figures, and sports became an important part of his life. He played baseball through college, and was later offered a minor-league contract by Branch Rickey, the general manager of the Cardinals. Hyland declined the offer, at the urging of his parents, who exerted a strong influence on their son.

A friend of Robert Hyland's (he never knew who) sent Hyland's photograph to Hollywood. He was offered movie contracts with Fox, Paramount and David O. Selznick, but turned them all down. "Against my parents' wishes, I went out to Hollywood, but they pulled me away from that."[21]

Hyland attended Saint Louis University, graduated with a degree in business, and decided on a career in radio. While at the university, he worked at station WEW in programming. He was also sports editor of the college newspaper, co-captain of the baseball team, and president of his junior and senior classes. "Radio was always my great love," he said years later. "It just grew on me, somehow. During my years at Saint Louis University, I knew what I wanted: a career in radio."[22]

Following graduation, Hyland entered the Navy and was commissioned as an ensign. He served until hay fever caused him to be medically discharged.

After the Navy, Hyland started his radio career in Quincy, Illinois, at WTAD. Years later he recalled, "I did everything, including sweep the studio. But I soon realized I wasn't cut out for reading livestock prices and weather reports — all the on-air work. All the real action seemed to be on the business side."[23]

Hyland returned to St. Louis in 1945 as an account executive at KXOK, and was named the sales manager at KXOK-FM in 1946. He left that position in 1950 to become an account executive at WBBM, the CBS-owned radio station in Chicago.

(Left to right) KMOX's Jim Butler, Bob Hyland and Mizzou head football coach, Don Faurot. *Hyland Family Archives*

The decision to move to Chicago was an easy one because "I had always wanted to become associated with CBS."[24] Network officials watched the young advertising executive quickly rise to first place on the sales staff.

In 1951, CBS moved Hyland to St. Louis to become KMOX's national sales manager. He was named general sales manager in November 1952, assistant general manager in June 1954, and replaced Eugene Wilke as general manager of KMOX in October 1955. CBS named him a network vice president in 1959, and continued to hold him in the very highest regard until his death in 1992. According to Nancy Widmann, president of the radio division of CBS in 1992, Hyland "was someone who was a total and complete visionary. If there was an idea that we were thinking about for radio ... the first person anyone at CBS would think about would be Bob Hyland."[25]

He was later named a senior vice president for the network, and on one occasion was offered the presidency of CBS Radio. It was an offer he turned down because of his deep commitment to the St. Louis community.

Hyland's name became synonymous with KMOX radio for the next forty years. Under his direction, KMOX radio became one of the most influential radio stations in the country and ranked among the top five stations, nationally, for many years.

In the fall of 1976, 26 percent of the St. Louis radio audience listened to KMOX during the day. The station's nearest competitor had a less than 9 percent share of the audience.[26]

Because of Hyland's successful programming innovations, CBS always considered KMOX the "jewel in the company's crown." This designation began with the company's founder and first chairman of the board, William Paley. According to Jack Buck, Paley was "so fond of Bob Hyland, he let him do whatever he wanted to do,"[27] because Hyland made more money for the network than even some of their owned and operated television stations.

Over the years, Hyland's lifestyle and work schedule became legendary. A *Wall Street Journal* article named him one of corporate America's most notorious workaholics. His radio station was his obsession. He would arrive at his office at about 3 a.m. and not leave until 6:30 or 7 p.m. He conducted business on the telephone in the wee hours of the morning, and had a reputation for always hanging up first. Every morning, very early, the newspapers were delivered to his office; after reading them, he would leave to attend Mass at the Old Cathedral. He personally answered every letter that came to KMOX. He monitored the station almost around-the-clock, and was known to make calls from his home with suggestions and complaints.

Rich Dalton, an intern from Southern Illinois University at Edwardsville in the early '70s recalls, "Mr. Hyland was always in control. In fact, I have never since worked at a place at which the boss had such an all-pervading presence."[28]

Each and every day, Hyland conducted a morning staff meeting to discuss, determine and plan the day's programming, knowing that if a news story made it necessary,

Robert F. Hyland Jr. in 1965. *Buzz Taylor Photography, Hyland Family Archives*

program content could be changed within minutes of air time. Any problems that might arise were explored and possible solutions were discussed. He understood that the product he was bringing to the people had to be adapted, modified and changed in days, minutes, and, sometimes, even seconds. This perceptive insight earned Hyland the highest respect from the KMOX audience. In a tribute to Hyland on the day of his death, one listener commented, "I admired him because he furnished this area with ... knowledge that the average person just doesn't read about. But if you listen to KMOX, you just have to know what is going on."[29]

Robert Hyland's distaste of television was renowned.

Bill Bidwill recalled his favorite story on KMOX's tribute to Hyland in March 1992. He said the legend was that when Hyland went to the new office downtown, the television set in his conference room was never hooked up. It was there, but it was never turned on — it was never plugged in to the wall.[30]

Rich Dalton remembers that although he hadn't even met him, one night he received a phone call from Hyland.

"I wrote a news story about a television tower that had fallen down. After it was broadcast, I got a phone call, 'Mr. Dalton, you're new here and probably didn't know that we don't mention the other media on KMOX. Next hour, when you rewrite the story, you will use the term broadcast tower *instead of* TV tower.' *The call came on the inside line, which meant it came from his office, and it was three in the morning!"[31]*

Many thought Hyland did not recognize television as a viable medium. Tom Kirgin remembers, "He had this thing about television because he was dedicated to radio ...

One of the jokes the salespeople got from Mr. Hyland was that 'surely it was never intended for pictures to fly through the air and materialize in your living room.'"[32]

Kevin Horrigan believed that,

"In [Hyland's] mind, he considered television a passing fancy ... that sooner or later people would come to their senses."[33]

However, even with all the jokes, in reality, television was Hyland's major competition. Wendy Wiese recalls,

"He would go after television when most radio people wouldn't begin to take on that kind of battle."[34]

And most of the time, KMOX and Hyland were successful.

Hyland expected loyalty from his employees, as Anthony Coleman of the KMOX staff said at the Hyland tribute in 1992,

"[Hyland] wanted his staff's loyalty to KMOX and commitment to the radio industry."[35]

Bob Hyland did not tolerate inefficiency or ineffectiveness. He set a good example, and expected others to follow his lead.

"I don't ask anyone to work any harder than I do. I set the pace, and I don't think anyone feels coerced or beaten. There's a lot of dedication and commitment at this station, and when you don't see it, it stands out like a sore thumb."[36]

Robert Hyland was once asked to describe his management philosophy and how that philosophy contributed to the success of KMOX Radio.

The first element was **Total Commitment.** *He explained that he believed in leadership by example. "If the leader of an organization shows that he is totally committed to its success … that attitude will permeate an entire organization."* **Urgency** *was the next element. "If an idea is worth implementing, it's worth implementing now." In explaining* **Versatility**, *Hyland said KMOX had four basic products — news, information, sports and entertainment, and the on-air people as well as behind-the-scenes personnel were "recruited and chosen with the goal of making them capable of dealing with two or more of these program elements."* **Aggressiveness** *was next on Hyland's list. "I am not content, and I do not permit our organization to be content, with anything but top performance in any area … KMOX Radio tries harder because it is number one and wants to stay there." Hyland's final element in his management philosophy was* **Team Spirit**. *"I believe it is the obligation and challenge of management to make sure that every member of his organization, from top to bottom, is imbued with the highest level of pride simply to be associated with that organization."*[37]

By utilizing these elements, under Hyland's management, KMOX's full potential for communication, information and community service was realized.

The station's commitment to serve the metropolitan area was evidenced by the tremendous amount of community involvement by Hyland, the station itself, and others on the staff. As Hyland told KMOX listeners in 1988,

"We are deeply involved in community affairs and many major community activities ... we're personally involved with RCGA, Downtown St. Louis, Muny Opera, St. Louis Zoo, Girl Scouts and Boy Scouts, St. Louis Symphony, Gateway Mall Task Force, July Fourth Celebration ... so you can see we're involved with the community in many varied ways and this way, in being involved with the community and the leaders, and being part of the city, we get a pulse of the city and what the people are thinking."[38]

Remembering Hyland, Bob Hardy observed,

"That was the kind of thing that rubbed off ... virtually every member of the staff ... by example from Bob Hyland ... have themselves gotten involved in specific charities and support of those charities as part of a commitment to the community. The community has allowed a good many of us, more than an ample opportunity to test our talents and to go as far in this profession as we care to go or want to go. And when a community does that, then you owe a little something back to the community for giving you that chance. And that's the philosophy that deals with KMOX Radio's commitment to St. Louis."[39]

Robert Hyland was a living example of the station's philosophy of community involvement. At the time of his death, he belonged to thirteen professional organizations, fifty-two civic groups, two academic societies, eight social clubs, and had received numerous honors and awards. Many people in the community agree that, over time, Robert Hyland probably had more of an influence on St. Louis than any mayor.

Bob Hardy –
The Road to "The Voice of St. Louis"

One of Bob Hardy's favorite sayings was, "Ya gotta be flexible." It was a saying that he applied to his daily life on a regular basis. Fortunately, in 1957, he broke his flexible rule. And by taking this once-in-a-lifetime inflexible stance, he soon became a household name in St. Louis, one of the city's best-loved broadcasters and, ultimately, the voice in "The Voice of St. Louis."

Hardy was born in May 1930 in DuBois, Pennsylvania, a small town in the northwestern part of the state. He was only two when his parents divorced. Moving to Syracuse, New York, his mother remarried, and he was legally adopted by Russell F. Hardy. The senior Hardy worked for the Syracuse *Herald-Journal*, where Bob learned to love current events and the news.

Hardy spent his summers as a boy around the Finger Lakes of upstate New York. During those summers, he learned to

Hardy, at five years old. *Hardy Family Archives*

play golf, a pastime that would remain a passion for him throughout his life. He also took flying lessons at the age of fifteen, and later, when he was in the Air Force, he earned his private pilot's license at Park's College through the Scott Aero Club.

Music also was an important part in Hardy's young life, another love that would continue throughout his lifetime. He was an accomplished pianist and had a band during high school.

At his high school graduation from Onondaga Valley Academy in Syracuse, he played George Gershwin's "Rhapsody in Blue" in its entirety and completely from memory.

In September 1948, he joined the Air Force and attended basic training at Lackland Air Force Base in San Antonio, Texas. From there he was assigned to Scott Air Force Base in Belleville, Illinois, to attend the Air Force's Radio School. The

Hardy and the future Mrs. Hardy, Rita A. Giering, at Scott Air Force Base in 1951. *Hardy Family Archives*

course was thirty-six weeks long, and after finishing near the top of his class, he remained at the base as an instructor. In 1950, in addition to teaching, he became a technician at the base radio station and was attached to the Armed Forces Radio Station Hospital Network. About this time, he started thinking about a career in the news field.

"There were some bad floods near East Alton, and I was one of the hundreds of GIs who were used for sandbagging. I described my experiences in a letter to my dad, who was a columnist for the Syracuse Herald-Journal, *and he liked it so much, he printed it. He urged me to do more writing. I gave it some thought."*[40]

According to Jim Butler, Hardy had his eye on KMOX even then.

"I worked the all-night record shift, and in '51 or '52, when Bob was stationed at Scott Air Force Base, he came over to the station one night about 1 a.m. He sat there for a couple of hours watching the operation. He was so impressed with everything. He told me several times over the years, that if it hadn't been for that night, he

The Hardy Family in 1967. From left, Sandy, Re, Bob and Bob Jr. *Hardy Family Archives*

probably wouldn't have thought so highly of KMOX."[41]

While at Scott, Hardy pursued his two passions — music and golf. He formed a band, and was very active in musical shows on base. It was his love of music that helped him meet the real love of his life. Rita Giering (although Hardy never called her anything but Re, saying Rita was just too long of a name!) was a member of the Women's Air Force and attending Radio School. She had done some professional singing and was auditioning for a stage production Hardy was putting together for the base. The couple was married in 1951, and their daughter, Sandra, was born in 1952. Robert Jr. was born in 1954.

Hardy was reassigned to Clark Air Force Base in the Philippine Islands in June 1952 — an unaccompanied tour for the first year. Subsequently, his wife and daughter joined him. While assigned to Armed Forces Radio at Clark as the chief

Bob Hardy interviews Rocky Marciano in 1953, during the boxer's visit to Clark Air Force Base in the Philippine Islands. *Hardy Family Archives*

Hardy's official Air Force photo from 1954. *U.S. Air Force*

engineer, he designed and supervised the construction of the base radio station. The design incorporated a new technical concept of placing all the wiring in a floor tunnel throughout the building. His other duties included servicing the Voice of America transmitter and a Baggio transmitter.

Given where Hardy ended up, it is ironic that the slogan for the Radio Station was "Information-Education-Entertainment."[42]

During his assignment at Clark, Hardy began doing newscasts and became a correspondent for the Armed Forces Radio Station network in Tokyo, Japan. He interviewed dignitaries traveling through the Philippines, as well as local politicians and celebrities. Some of his early interviews included Philippine President Ramon Magsaysay, Vice President Richard Nixon, boxer Rocky Marciano, band leader Xavier Cugat, singer Abby Lane, and baseball great Ed Mathews.

While at Clark, Hardy conducted what could very well have been

Hardy (left) hosting an "At Your Service"-type program for the Armed Forces Radio Station at Clark AFB in 1954. *Hardy Family Archives*

*the very **first** "At Your Service" program. Seated around the dining room table in a private home on Clark Air Force Base, Hardy conducted an on-air show, "A Word To The Wives," with three guests answering questions put to them.*

In addition, Hardy, known as "Bobbin Bob," was the disc jockey for the sign-on "Musical Clock" show each morning. He also wrote a weekly newspaper article called "of mikes and men," a practice he continued for a brief period when he returned from the Philippines in 1955.

In his spare time at Clark, Hardy served as the master of ceremonies for military and civilian functions. He also formed and led the "Top Flighters," a fourteen-piece, all-airman dance band that performed throughout the area.

While at Clark, Hardy took the test for Officer Candidate School. He had decided to make the military his first career, and go into a news career later. He passed the test and was accepted for OCS, but was not given an entry date.

In June 1955, Hardy received orders and returned to Scott Air Force Base as a radio instructor. Upon his return to Scott, he was told that he would not be going to OCS at that time because the Air Force needed him as an instructor. His flexible, stay-loose attitude took over, and he took a part-time job with WIBV Radio in Belleville. For two years, Hardy worked the 6 a.m. to 3 p.m. shift at WIBV, and the 4 p.m. to midnight shift at Scott.

Early in 1957, he received orders, not to OCS, but to the Dew Line in Greenland — another unaccompanied tour. As much as he loved the military, he would not leave his family, again. He refused to be flexible, used sixty days of built-up leave, and after nine years of service in the Air Force, accepted an honorable discharge.

Hardy took a job as news director with WIL in St. Louis in July 1957. WIL was one of only six radio stations in St. Louis at the time (a number that has grown to well over forty today). Hardy's job included hourly newscasts and street reporting, along with hosting functions and presenting speeches throughout the community. Under his directorship, "Action

Central News" became a hit, but it was not the type of news coverage Hardy wanted to do. He believed the future of radio news lay in serious, classic, in-depth style reporting, the way he wanted to cover the stories.

In March 1960, Hardy conducted an exclusive interview with a convicted rapist. Ronald Lee Wolfe had been sentenced to die in the Missouri gas chamber only hours before the interview. Wolfe refused to speak to anyone in the press except Hardy, who visited the condemned man in his cell at the Pike County Jail in Bowling Green, Missouri. The next day, WIL aired the interview which had been incorporated into a series of documentaries looking at capital punishment.

The new broadcasting concept across town at KMOX radio was just the type of programming Hardy was looking for. But

Hardy as WIL news director (standing, from left) with Eagle Scouts Frank Vielhaber, James Reed, and (seated) George Akers Jr. *Edward H. Goldberger*

before he had a chance to go to Bob Hyland, Hyland came to him. The tenacious news director at WIL had caught the attention of KMOX insiders and, specifically, Hyland's son, Rip. Everyone knew Hardy could make the new "At Your Service" an even bigger success. In 1992, Hardy reminisced about how he came to be hired at KMOX back in 1960.

"Bob Hyland called me down from WIL where I was the news director, doing Action Central News reading twenty-two lines a minute ... along with Jack Carney who was playing records there in both the morning and the afternoon drive times — Jack and I went back a long, long way. But Bob Hyland called me down and he said, 'My son Rip thinks you might be a good addition to KMOX Radio. Would you be interested in working here?' And there I am in that sanctified hall he called an office and I said, 'Yeah, sure, boy, if there's anything anybody in broadcasting would want to do it would be to go to KMOX.' He said, 'All right, I want you to start April 17. Now take a vacation.' This was about March 25. I said, 'A vacation?' He said, 'Yeah, it's bad weather around here, go to

Hardy's professional photo from 1963. *Hardy Family Archives*

Florida, take the family to Florida.' And he got up ... and reached over and shook my hand and I walked out and went to Florida with my wife and two kids. And about five days into sitting on the beach down there at St. Petersburg, I suddenly asked myself, 'My God, what have you done? You've shaken a guy's hand who's guaranteed you a job but you have nothing on paper' ... so I called. He wouldn't take the call but his secretary did and said, 'Oh, yes he's expecting you to come into work on the 17th of April.' So somewhat relieved, I spent the rest of the vacation with my family down there and came back ... and reported for work at eight o'clock on that April 17th. I walked into Mr. Hyland's office. He welcomed me to KMOX and I said, 'Well, I wasn't sure I really had a job.' He said, 'Well, you do. Rex Davis is off today, I want you to do the 12 o'clock news.' Well, my God, the 12 o'clock news back in 1960 was a major newscast. I can't remember, I think it was sponsored by either Standard Oil or Monroe Shock Absorbers, and to be called upon on your first day to do a major newscast was enough to make you quake in your boots. And I did, I was shook."[43]

Hardy also recalled being told that the job was a temporary position.

"Mr. Hyland said I should always remember the job was a trial kind of thing. He wanted me full-time, but it was temporary and whether or not it would be permanent would depend on how I progressed. On my thirtieth anniversary I walked in here at five o'clock in the morning ... in comes the boss with a beautiful cake — Bob Hardy, thirty years, all that sort of thing. And I said, 'Thank you very much Mr. Hyland, I really appreciate it.' He said, 'Remember what I told you the day you came here — I told you it was a temporary job. I want you to know it still is!'"[44]

Hardy loved the job at KMOX. He was given every opportunity to perfect his craft and he did just that. He became an expert in bringing the listeners what they wanted and needed to know, being referred to as "the dean of talk radio hosts in St. Louis."[45] In addition to his daily anchoring duties, he wrote numerous major documentaries and covered every national political convention, beginning in 1964. He became an expert on election coverage, and although election days were long, he never missed one.

His objectivity and integrity earned him the respect of many. In fact, he was so objective in his reporting that Jim Butler said of Hardy,

"Bob could have a liberal Democrat accuse him of being a hard-shell Republican, and almost in the same breath, he would have a hard-shell Republican accuse him of being a liberal Democrat. He understood the values of objectivity in this business."[46]

Hardy was a master of the "At Your Service" concept. He and his guests shared a mutual respect for one another. Guests on the show knew Hardy would be fair and honest with them — even when asking the tough questions. He learned early on that the best way to conduct a radio talk show was to listen. He often said that most interviewers will work their way down a list of questions, but fail to pay attention to the answers. His technique was to have a list of about ten questions, pick the best one, and throw the rest out! Having to listen and ask questions on the spot made his job more difficult, but it worked. Bob Hardy was the best of the best. His colleagues concurred.

Jim White recalls Hardy being his teacher without even knowing it, as White worked with him and learned from him.

Charles Brennan remembered that Hardy was always prepared.

"He could 'wing it' with the best of them, but he didn't. Broadcasting was a serious responsibility to Bob ... he made each of us reach a little higher."[47]

Bob Hardy died in 1993. During a tribute to him, Senator Thomas Eagleton said,

"Bob had a remarkable ability to get behind a headline and really get into the meaning and significance of the news story ... not everyone can do the substance behind the headline — Bob Hardy could."[48]

Senior White House correspondent for *Newsweek* magazine, Tom DeFrank recalled,

"Bob was 'Mr. KMOX.' He personified to me professionalism and integrity.... I can never remember a situation where he was flustered

or lost his composure or balance, and I can never remember a situation where he didn't give every listener, every caller, every guest, an opportunity to have his or her say."[49]

One of Hardy's regular guests, Jordan Goodman, *Money* magazine's Wall Street correspondent, remembered,

"Bob could always draw out of me what the audience wanted ... and I think I became a better journalist by [being on the air with him].... Bob never lost touch with the audience."[50]

Asked once how many guests he had hosted on KMOX, Hardy couldn't even begin to count, but he had no trouble remembering some of his favorites. The list included Hubert Humphrey, Cardinal Joseph Ritter, Cardinal John Carberry, Admiral Elmo Zumwalt, Rosalyn Carter, and his number one favorite, the late Gussie Busch Jr.

Hardy tried his hand at television on KMOX-TV, Channel 4 in September 1967, much to everyone's amazement, given Hyland's feelings toward that medium. Hardy was on with Fred Porterfield doing the Sunday evening news. He decided though, that television was not to his liking, and gave it up in quick order. That move also amazed many, but not the ones who knew him best.

Said Bob Costas of Hardy, "I've seldom encountered someone who was as happy and secure in his own place ... KMOX was where he wanted to be. He loved his home and his family and his working circumstances, and I think when someone has that kind of security, they're able to appreciate the people around them ... and the paths the lives of those people take, without any resentment, but simply with appreciation and with a certain kind of love for them. Bob was sort of an emotional anchor for the station. This is a business where people have a lot of insecurities and where personalities are sometimes mercurial. He was a rock in that respect, he knew who he was and he was secure in who he was, and people when they were around him tended to be a little more calm and sure of themselves because they could count on him."[51]

Hardy helped KMOX attain many firsts. He was the host of the first radio bridge, a monthly satellite link between KMOX and Moscow Radio. His live broadcasts from five Eastern

European capitals in five days set new standards in the broad-cast industry, and culminated in a National Headliner Award for himself and the station. He traveled to Saudi Arabia to broadcast the first live satellite linkup between KMOX listeners and the troops during the Persian Gulf War. The programs allowed the troops to talk directly to their families at home.

Bob Costas believes one reason Hardy was so successful was,

"He had one of the best deliveries for a newsman on the radio that I have ever heard, because it was simultaneously authoritative and warm. He could be conversational and yet have that classic old style radio sound all at the same time. And he projected authority without arrogance. He sounded well informed without ever posing as an expert. He never talked down to the audience. He was never 'let me show off everything I know about this topic,' but he always was well prepared for everything he did and when he did those open lines ... he could punctuate each idea yet maintain his own integrity and objectivity while at the same time engage the callers.... It was a broadcasting asset."[52]

Businesses in the St. Louis community appreciated Hardy's talents, using him as their spokesman on several promotional tapes and sales videos used worldwide. He enjoyed doing them all, but his love of flying made the McDonnell Douglas promotions among his favorites.

Another reason Hardy was so successful and loved by so many was his humility. He was the same person on-the-air as off-the-air, a rare quality in the business. When Hardy had a stroke in 1991, his doctors wanted him to stay at home and not go back to work for at least eight weeks. He was having trouble speaking, and had very little use of his right hand. After three weeks he was feeling fine, but still not speaking as clearly as he had before the stroke. He decided it was time to go back to work because he felt he could be an example to other stroke victims. He wanted people to realize that if he could come back on the air, even though not quite 100 percent, others could also move ahead after a stroke.

The St. Louis community genuinely liked Hardy and con-

As radio announcer Bob Hardy describes the action among the aerialists of the Big Top, Mary Lou Atwell listens enthralled. Guided by Hardy's words, she "sees" two

They "watched," although blind, with

Betty Pollards, Bob Schmidt and Tony Delgado (adults, left to right) were three of the 10 Telephone Pioneers who took the kids to the show

St. Louis Telephone Pioneers and a skilled radio broadcaster have proved that it's not necessary to be able to see to enjoy the circus.

For the second straight year, the Pioneers brought a group of children from the Missouri School for the Blind to the Ringling Brothers-Barnum & Bailey show at the St. Louis Arena.

While the performers flew through the air, put ferocious lions and tigers through their paces, or brought a chuckle with the clown acts, KMOX announcer Bob Hardy served as the "eyes" of 65 children listening through headsets the Pioneers provided. These pictures show what the guests "saw" and how they reacted.

Hardy describing the action of the circus performers for students of the Missouri School for the Blind in 1976. *St. Louis Post-Dispatch*

handsome men, two lovely women fly from one trapeze to another—and finally a third man executes a triple somersault in midair.

the greatest of ease

Mary Lou's twin, Mary Ann Atwell, and their brother, Ted, are thrilled by the prowess of Gretchen, the lioness, who, at right, leaps through a flaming hoop held by Wolfgang Holzmair.

Hardy and a pal, promoting the Illinois Farm Bureau in 1979. *Hardy Family Archives*

sidered him a member of their own family. He reciprocated by sharing himself with them. His audiences knew all about his family, his farm "Wildflower," the bees he kept until his stroke, his love of music, boating, flying, golfing, and snow-skiing, which he took up at the age of fifty-eight.

Hardy considered himself very lucky and credited the community's support for his success, always believing that he must give something in return.

In September 1975, the Ringling Brothers-Barnum & Bailey Circus performed at the Arena. Sixty-five children from the Missouri School for the Blind "saw" the show as Bob Hardy became their "eyes" for the evening. The children were provided special headsets by the St. Louis Telephone Pioneers, a group of past and present telephone employees. Hardy, giving a creative narration of what was happening during the entire show, said the job was a challenge — "How can you describe an elephant? You say it's as big as your dad's car, with four legs like tree trunks and skin like leather" — but well-worth it "When I sit here and see those grins and see them clapping, I know I'm getting through."[53]

Throughout his career, Hardy received honors and awards from more than fifty media, civic and service organizations. These include the *Associated Press, United Press International*, Missouri Broadcasters, The George Foster Peabody Award, The Abe Lincoln Award and the Daughters of the American Revolution Medal of Honor; as well as honors from Southern Illinois University at Edwardsville, Dartmouth College, McKendree College and the United States Air Force.

Hardy was a past chairman of the board of the Southern Illinois University Foundation at Edwardsville, a past president of the St. Louis Press Club, member of the board of directors of the James S. McDonnell USO, member of the public relations committee of the St. Louis Heart Association, and a member of the Sigma Delta Chi Society of Professional Journalists.

Hardy was active in the Shriners, which he joined in 1963, and was deeply committed to the Crippled Children's Hospital. He was elected Potentate of Ainad Temple in 1976 and served on the Imperial Shrine Public Relations Committee for many years. He was also a 33rd degree Mason.

Bob Hardy was a true professional who became known and respected, both nationally and internationally, in his profession. He challenged his listeners to learn, and with his help, they did. By reporting the facts and allowing his listeners to make up their own minds, his standards became ones that continue to be emulated by others in the field.

Robert Hyland
Sets the Groundwork

In the early 1950s, entertainment was still the name of the game. But as the decade advanced, the station began to turn in a new direction — a step necessitated by the popularity of a new medium called television. For radio to survive, the emphasis would have to turn away from entertainment and move toward news, information and sports.

One of Hyland's first acts as new general manager was to add Cardinal baseball to station programming. In the past, the station had broadcast games, but the entire schedule had not been aired for fifteen years. The new broadcast team included Harry Caray, Joe Garagiola and Jack Buck, representing experience at the mike and on the field. By including Cardinal baseball on KMOX, the station was starting to serve the local community. Said Hyland years later about his decision to broadcast baseball on KMOX, "I believed then, and believe now, that radio's strength lies in becoming an increasingly local medium. And sports is one of the best ways to capture local loyalty."[54] Cardinal baseball on KMOX was soon followed by local professional and college football and basketball, plus numerous sports specials.

The informative, but mainly entertaining, Housewives Protective League, was headed in the right direction, but definitely not what Hyland had in mind.

Each CBS-owned and -operated radio station had its own on-air personality talking for a half hour each day about things of interest to homemakers. KMOX had Lee Adams and then Grant Williams. According to Jim Butler, these were never the host's real name, but a name made up by CBS using names from U.S. history and the Civil War. As an example, Robert E. Lee and John Quincy Adams became Lee Adams.[55]

Hyland's philosophy that people should be educated while being entertained, led to the increase of informational programming and local service. In 1956, KMOX became the first commercial radio station in the country to offer a college credit course in prime time. As many stations were gearing their programming to the teen music audience, KMOX, in cooperation with Washington University, offered credit in a music appreciation course to listeners who fulfilled the course requirements. Seventy-four people from fourteen states completed the course. By 1958, KMOX had more than 2,000 "lis-

Dr. Thomas A. Dooley (left) talks about a broadcast with Rex Davis, public affairs director, in 1956. *KMOX*

tener students." The course offerings included "Critical Issues in Public Schools" and "Child Psychology" (co-sponsored with Southern Illinois University), "Current Social Programs" (Saint Louis University) and "Successful Money Management" (Saint Louis University's School of Commerce and Finance).

A 1956 KMOX series taped in Laos by Dr. Thomas Dooley, a young St. Louis doctor, was initially intended for local audiences but soon gained national attention. "That Free Men May Live" was a weekly feature from the Communist-threatened country in order to promote a better understanding between Americans and Laotians. Dr. Dooley was in Laos as the head of a four-man, independent, medical-diplomatic mission sponsored by the International Rescue Committee. They set up emergency hospitals to serve disease-plagued villages and

Dr. Dooley visits with natives of Vang Vieng, Laos, where his emergency hospital was located. Dooley's series, "That Free Men May Live," was recorded in villages throughout the country for KMOX. *KMOX*

training clinics to school the Laotians in sanitation and mid-wife procedures.

Dooley's reports were taped in remote mountain villages, carried down from the mountains by Jeep or on foot to Vientiane, and then flown 9,000 miles to St. Louis. The reports described in graphic and dramatic detail "his efforts to translate, on a person-to-person basis, the ideals of democracy."[56] The quality and importance of the contents of the program was confirmed when the State Department requested copies for their own use.

In April 1957, after twenty-five years in the former Mart Building, KMOX moved to an interim location at Ninth and Sydney streets. The move was accomplished without broadcast interruption, and would serve station operations until a new permanent facility was completed for CBS Radio in St.

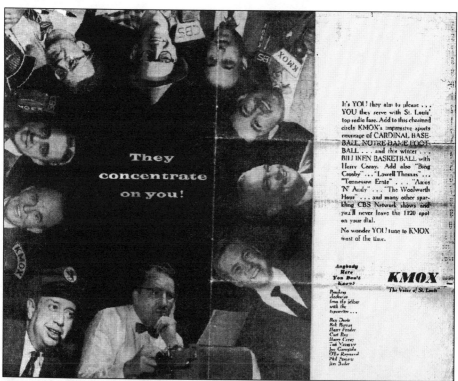

KMOX personalities featured in a 1957 ad include Rex Davis, Bob Burnes, Harry Fender, Curt Ray, Harry Caray, Ted Mangner, Joe Garagiola, Ollie Raymand, Phil Stevens and Jim Butler. *KMOX*

Louis.

The year 1957 also brought "The Voice of St. Louis" a National Headliner Club Silver Medallion for Outstanding Public Service by a Radio Station for its program on juvenile delinquency, "Youth in the Shadows." The award was the first ever given to a radio station in the twenty-two-year history of the Headliner competition.

Cardinal baseball broadcasts continued for the third consecutive year, and more than 130 nights of the year were devoted to fully-sponsored live play-by-play baseball, football and basketball.

The daily programming during 1957 was very popular with listeners. It included "The Clockwatcher," with Ted Mangner and Jim Butler in the morning; "The Jack Buck Show," a late afternoon talk and recorded music program; and "The Harry Fender Show," from the Steeplechase Room of the Chase Hotel, late at night. These programs were teamed with the CBS Radio Network offerings — Arthur Godfrey, the Ford Road shows, daytime dramatic serials, Art Linkletter, Jack Benny, "Amos 'n Andy," and "Gunsmoke" — and garnered KMOX an 84.4 percent share of the audience in the ratings.[57]

As the philosophy of local service and informational radio continued to grow at KMOX, the station focused on specific community problems and needs, as they became apparent. One such public service program focused on the Conelrad weather warning system. The FCC approved KMOX's "Operation Weather Alert" proposal in December 1957, providing a faster, more effective way of broadcasting information about tornadoes and other severe weather conditions. "The Voice of St. Louis" would broadcast the Conelrad weather alert signals indicating emergency weather, direct from the United States Weather Bureau, and make them available for rebroadcast by all radio and television stations in the area. In addition, the station presented a complete public educational program to familiarize residents with the new system and procedures in the event of severe weather conditions. Two awards were presented to KMOX for its "Operation Weather Alert": the Air

Force Chief of Staff Award and the National Safety Council's Public Interest Award.

Children were an important part of the audience for "The Voice of St. Louis" in 1957. To serve the young listeners, the station started a new program called "A Visit With Kitty." The program consisted of children's music and stories for thirty minutes, and then fifteen minutes of French lessons with "Mademoiselle Jeanette." The lessons, presented in conjunction with the St. Louis Board of Education, were geared to a second grade level, but were beneficial in the primary and secondary grades as well as for adults working on French pronunciation. At the end of 1957, there were over five hundred "class members."

Hyland's community service radio station continued to take shape into the new year. A new public affairs program, "Challenge 58," was hosted by two well-known newsmen in the area — Rex Davis, KMOX news director, and Richard Amberg, *St. Louis Globe-Democrat* publisher. The weekly informal discussion fostered a better understanding of the local, regional, and national news, and contributed toward the move away from pure entertainment.

During 1958, KMOX became the first CBS-owned radio or television station to broadcast locally originated editorials. The first program in the series, "KMOX Radio Takes a Stand," dealt with fluoridation of county water.

Hyland said at the time of his new series, "KMOX's role in the editorial field is just beginning ... and we will broadcast subsequent editorials as the need arises ... and when the interest of the public will be served."[58]

Hyland's editorials were always his own ideas, but were written by Alice Koch English, KMOX's program director. During the editorial broadcast on June 23, 1958, KMOX became the first broadcasting station to endorse a candidate for public office.

In October 1958, the St. Louis Baseball Cardinals traveled to the Orient for a month-long tour. KMOX's decision to broadcast seven of their overseas games precipitated another first in

WE'VE GOT
RADIOS
FOR KMOX

LISTENERS

Bob Anthony   Jack Buck   Bob Burnes

Jim Butler   Harry Caray   Rex Davis

Harry Fender   Joe Garagiola   Jack Hill

Kitty   Ted Mangner   Doug Newman

1120 ON YOUR DIAL "THE *Choice* OF ST. LOUIS"

Roy Queen   Ollie Raymand   Steve Rowan

Grant Williams   Paul Wills

In celebration of National Radio Month KMOX Radio personalities will award four radios a day to KMOX listeners every day, May 2 through 31. Listen to KMOX Radio for complete National Radio Month contest details. Tune in to your favorite KMOX programs for daily winners.

KM⊙X CBS
RADIO

An April 1958 ad. *KMOX*

the station's history, and a wire message to Robert Hyland from then Vice President Richard M. Nixon stated:

"In my opinion, there is no better way of strengthening mutual understanding among nations than through the people-to-people approach, and I am convinced that international sports engagements are playing an important role in building international friendship and good will. For that reason, I particularly appreciate this opportunity to congratulate KMOX radio and all those responsible for broadcasting the games which the St. Louis Cardinals will be playing in Japan..." [59]

The station's programming in 1959 contributed even more to the community. Special features included "The Bottom of the Bottle," a compelling look at alcoholics in Missouri and Illinois; "They'll Never Walk Alone," a moving report of how the United Cerebral Palsy Association helps those afflicted with the disease; and "The Velvet Curtain," an investigation of the problems of the aged in Missouri.

Regularly scheduled features included "The Decision is

The station's new home at Hampton and Wise avenues as of August 1959.
Alice Koch English

Yours," presenting both sides of a current and controversial civic issue, and "Operation Job-Hunt," stressing the importance of hiring high school and college students during the summer to employers.

On August 31, 1959, KMOX moved into the nation's most "modern" radio station with all of the latest broadcasting equipment. The 15,500-square-foot complex, located at the corner of Hampton and Wise avenues, was designed specifically for KMOX. The building had the distinction of being the first radio-only facility built by CBS in twenty years. According to Hyland, that fact "demonstrates the faith of the Columbia Broadcasting System in the dynamic future of radio and the equally dynamic future of our growing city. Despite its pride in its pace-setting new facilities, KMOX continues broadcasting with a great sense of humility…. A radio station, to be worthy of the name, is the sum of the wholesome entertainment, compelling features, reliable news, and, above all, active and responsible good citizenship."[60]

Settled into their new home, Hyland knew the time was right to take KMOX into a new era.

Hyland's Vision

In 1960, radio was beginning to lose the attention of an audience that for years had tuned in for entertainment. Advertisers, who once invested in radio time, were now turning to television. For radio to survive the challenge of the new medium, it would have to change its image and broaden its function. It was time to bring radio to adulthood.

Robert Hyland believed his colleagues were misjudging radio's potential adult audience and underestimating their intelligence and desire to know and learn. He believed that radio needed programming with a purpose; namely, to educate, to inform, and to become the voice of the community. He remarked at the time, "Radio has a duty to lead rather than follow public tastes — to become a focal point for the exchange of ideas and information."[61] He hired a market research group to test talk radio as a format. They came back with bad news: three out of four people said they wouldn't listen to it. KMOX conducted its own studies which resulted in findings echoing Hyland's beliefs: housewives didn't want to be talked down to, and men and women alike wanted to be informed about their community and the world around them. In short, people wanted to get information from the radio.

As a result of Hyland's beliefs and the audiences' desires, a startling and sensational programming change occurred, dominated entirely by Hyland's philosophy and dreams. It was a daring move that led to the birth of "At Your Service"

Hyland's new programming concept is promoted in February 1960. *KMOX*

and the beginning of talk radio.

Jack Buck recalls the name for the new program, "At Your Service," was one he suggested to Hyland. Buck had come to KMOX from Columbus, Ohio, where the title was being used for a radio program. He thought it would be perfect for the new programming concept Hyland was initiating.

During the now-legendary staff meeting on February 16, 1960, Hyland informed the KMOX personnel of the upcoming changes.

"To put it drastically," Hyland told his staff, "we are not going to have records on KMOX from 12 noon until 7 at night on a weekday … and this is something that will probably cause national attention to [KMOX]. It's going to be all-informative … but we're going to make the information such that it will be interesting, and attention-getting…. We are going to have approximately seventy outstanding people in St. Louis, of which six of the seventy will be called regulars. In other words they will appear on here once every two weeks…. [Guests] will be quizzed by Jack Buck on topics of the day … then listeners will be able to call in and ask these people questions on the subject matter that has been discussed."[62]

Hyland read to the staff the KMOX press release announcing the innovative schedule:

They were making the changes *"because [KMOX] does not choose to limit its prime afternoon time to the music that a home record player can provide. Complete dependence on recorded music in key audience time is easy programming — a crutch, and not representative of the full service that a station with complete facilities like KMOX can provide. Instead, KMOX believes it is time to give [the audience] programming with more substance and meaning; programming that is provocative and informative. We have confidence that our advertisers … will be eager to place their messages within this kind of attention-getting programming."*[63]

Hyland told his staff the changes were not meant to be sensational or to gain attention, but rather it was *"a belief that we've been thinking about for six months, off and on for six months, to try to make this station a better station, to try to make this station the station that it should be … and I assure you, you will be the talk of the country. If it fails, it fails, we'll try something else. But at least we're off our fannies and we're trying something…. I have every confidence it's going to work."*[64]

In a Pete Rahn column (*Globe-Democrat's* TV-Radio editor) dated February 18, 1960, Hyland described "At Your Service" as an:

"all-information format designed to broaden and widen the scope and function of radio during peak afternoon audience time…. Management of KMOX believes it is time that the housewife and homebound motorist be given programming with more substance, meaning and imagination … programming that is truly provocative, timely and informative…. The program will be a true newspaper of the air."[65]

Hyland's announcement was so drastic that the move was reported all over the country in publications such as *The Wall Street Journal, Advertising Age , Broadcasting, Billboard,* and *Variety* magazines.

Just eleven days before the February 29 debut of "At Your Service," Pete Rahn wondered in his column how the local audience would respond to KMOX's new format. No one at the time knew what a success it would be, only that everyone in the radio industry, both locally and nationally, would be watching closely. The move that some had called "Hyland's folly"[66] would turn out to be an idea whose time had come, the beginning of talk radio across the country.

At 3 p.m. on February 29, 1960, radio history was made as "At Your Service" took to the airwaves for its debut. The show's very first guest was St. Louis Mayor Raymond R. Tucker, hosted by Jack Buck. The program began with comments from Robert Hyland, general manager of KMOX and vice president of CBS.

"Ladies and Gentlemen, the program you are about to hear represents a new concept in afternoon programming for American radio — a concept we believe will set the pattern for radio broadcasting in this exciting new decade of the '60s. The program is called 'At Your Service' and is designed to be at the service of you thousands of listeners who want the full range of entertainment and information

from radio listening. The first hour will give you, the listener, an opportunity to question the top civic and opinion leaders of our city, the state and the nation. We're extremely proud that the first guest on our inaugural program is the great mayor of St. Louis, one of America's most outstanding mayors, His Honor Mayor Raymond R. Tucker.

The second hour will be as new, exciting and meaningful as we can make it. The KMOX Radio microphone will take you all over our listening area to bring you the stories behind the day's news and to bring you the best in educational, informative and entertainment features. We will welcome your comments and suggestions on 'At Your Service.' It's your program, and we will strive to tailor it to your needs and interests. And now, back to your 'At Your Service' host, Jack Buck."[67]

The program started with a fifteen-minute interview between Buck and the mayor, after which KMOX invited listeners to phone in their questions or comments. The show was a huge success!

Many said the concept wouldn't work, that the show would be "the biggest bomb ever laid by a local station,"[68] *that people only listened to the radio to be entertained.*

The critics argued that housewives wanted good music to

"soothe the day's little crises…. Never, never will this hard-working gal take time out to concentrate on a weighty discourse of a political or civic nature."[69]

But the "At Your Service" format — designed as a forum for the exchange of ideas, facts and opinions, and allowing dialogue between listeners and the experts — was a major triumph for "The Voice of St. Louis." Others in the industry quickly recognized the impact the new format would have. Only two weeks after the first "At Your Service" program, *Variety* reported that the "bold, new concept in afternoon radio programming … probably will have a snowballing effect on the program formats of major radio stations across the country."[70] Within months of the first "At Your Service" program, representatives from the major stations visited KMOX to study the operation, and KMOX's ratings soared within the first few months. Additionally, the station was recognized with several awards. Early in 1960, the station won three separate national awards in less than one month for its public affairs programming. Since its inception in 1960, the format has been adopted by over 2,000 radio stations in the United States and around the world, including Japan, Australia, Canada, Germany, the Netherlands and Mexico.

As with any new idea, a few things needed improving. At first, the sound on the phone lines was not the best. Within a short period of time, however, the quality was enhanced and callers sounded as if they were in the studio asking their questions in person.

One minor problem was that some hosts were having difficulty coming up with good questions for their guests. The solution, however, was an easy one.

John Sabin, who worked in the news room was asked by then program director, George Clare, to write a series of questions for the hosts of "At Your Service." "My contribution to 'At Your Service' was providing an integrated series of fifteen to twenty questions of no more than one line each for the hosts, so that the program provided the public with a specific or a general topic. In other words, if the guest was the mayor, the questions would ask about city hall and what is happening or ask about the police department and their regular patrols. This helped the hosts have basic questions that they then embellished upon with their own ideas so that the program became their own." Sabin provided the questions for the first month.[71]

The listeners had plenty of questions of their own.

According to Alice Koch English, "'At Your Service' picked up steam very, very quickly and it became the forum for St. Louis and for the whole region, and it continues to be."[72]

During the first week of broadcasts, KMOX's trunk lines were completely tied up with phone calls, with overflow calls jamming the exchange. People liked being able to get on the radio and express their opinions. J. Roy McCarthy screened and paraphrased the phoned-in questions and comments for the guests, and his talent and audience rapport kept the program fast-paced and lively.

Jim Butler, as the first executive producer of "At Your Service," was responsible for the guest lineup. The job became full time as the program's popularity grew, but getting guests was never, even in the beginning, difficult for the station. All the big names in St. Louis wanted to be on the air, which included Mayor Tucker, Senator Stuart Symington, Senator Thomas Hennings, Bing Devine, general manager of the St. Louis Baseball Cardinals, Governor James T. Blair, Police Chief Curtis Brostron, F.B.I. Chief Calvin Howard, and Ben Kerner, owner of the St. Louis Hawks basketball team.

The second hour of the "At Your Service" program proved as popular as the first. The days of "rip-and-read" news reporting ended as a new era of actualities and interviews began. Jack Buck continued as coordinator, bringing the events of the day and the names in the news through reports from Bob Hardy and the news department staff, and by using KMOX's new mobile microphone.

Hyland had procured new equipment that was perfect for field reporting because it had an almost studio quality. This quality was important to Hyland because it was just one more way of showing that KMOX was **the** *information station.*

KMOX personalities featured in the second "At Your Service" hour included Bob Holt, the "man of a thousand voices"; Bob Goddard, *St. Louis Globe-Democrat* columnist; John McCormick, the "man who walks and talks at midnight"; Steve Rowan, KMOX night news editor; and Ted Malone. Others featured periodically included Rex Davis, news editor; fashion expert, Miss Nanette; Laurent Torno, one of the Midwest's leading musical experts; and Dr. Alfred Weber of Saint Louis University.

The time frame from 5 to 7 p.m. was divided into news segments and features, as well as sports information with Bob Burnes and Harry Caray. The program consisted of locally produced news and CBS Network features, keeping the "At Your Service" theme alive for the rush-hour mobile audience as well as the late afternoon home audience.

It was during this time segment, on a sports program with Bob Burnes, that it was decided a delay button was necessary. "At Your Service" had been on for a couple of months. One night, a male caller got on the air with Burnes and said a choice four-letter word. The next day, the station's engineers built a delay mechanism. There had never been anything like it on the market, and nobody on any station had ever thought to make one. It began as a three-second delay, then went to a seven-second delay. In February 1965, the delay was reduced to 4 1/2 seconds to improve broadcast quality.[73]

In 1988, on the 28th anniversary of "At Your Service," Hyland joined Hardy, Wendy Wiese and Bill Wilkerson on the morning show, "Total Information," to talk about the original idea of "At Your Service." The conversation was rebroadcast in 1992.

"It was a great dream but we had great confidence in it. There were a lot of people in the industry that got a big kick out of it, said it will never work, it'll never happen, won't go more than thirty days and you'll be gone and your idea will be gone. But that didn't happen. We had great faith in the American public and that's really what it is, it's an interchange with the American public. The original idea was the fact that radio in those days had to do something because its audiences, its big shows, its soap operas were all going to television — so in order to stem the tide, in other words, you had to be creative on your own. You could either go one of two ways — you could play records or you could be creative another way and try to seek new ways to program your station, and that's what we did ... we felt there was another role for KMOX. KMOX was a traditional station that had been a mainstay in broadcasting. We felt there had to be a new thing come about in the broadcasting industry and we felt the people, this time, wanted to communicate, they wanted to talk to their government leaders and their health leaders, and law and so forth, and they'd like to know, they wanted to be informed and we thought this was just the right time and it turned out it was the right time."[74]

By January 1962, KMOX had included the Saturday 8 a.m.

to noon slot in its "programming-with-a-purpose" format. Next, weekday morning drive-time music was replaced by talk. Sunday morning programming followed. Hyland had succeeded in creating the idea that if something was of interest to mainstream St. Louis, not only was it on KMOX, but it was on KMOX more and better than anywhere else. The listeners responded. They wanted information, which was just what "The Voice of St. Louis" was giving them. Even in the mid- and late-morning programming, which continued as music, the shows became unique, with more information about the artists and songs.

It is noteworthy that since its programming change in 1960, KMOX has been one of the nation's most listened-to radio stations, consistently ranking number one in the St. Louis market, often with as high as a 48 percent share of the audience, and, at one time, a 53 percent share.

What factors account for the program's popularity and success? Were the people of St. Louis just ready for more news and knowledge? Or was it simply time for something new and different? We may never know. But we do know that "The Voice of St. Louis" responds to the voices of St. Louis, and those voices dictate the programming. As Robert Hyland liked to remind his staff, "Listeners are the most important ones of all. Listeners are what we're all about."[75]

"At Your Service" –
How It Worked

Although KMOX Radio depended on its on-air personalities to draw in the listeners, the concept of "At Your Service" could never have worked without the guests. Robert Hyland spent hours dreaming up ideas for shows, and determining who the people were that the listeners wanted to hear. Over the years there have been thousands who have appeared on the air. They include impressive names such as Eleanor Roosevelt, Gloria Steinem, Margaret Mead, Billy Graham, Jerry Lewis, Supreme Court Justice William O. Douglas, Senator Hubert Humphrey, Patrick Buchanan, Art Buchwald, Governors George Wallace, Jimmy Carter and Ronald Reagan; and British historian Arnold Toynbee, who was amazed that a local truck driver was familiar with his books. Guest experts have included pediatricians, marriage counselors, clergymen, teachers, scientists, gardeners, psychiatrists, plumbers, judges, veterinarians, visiting diplomats, hair stylists, chefs, philosophers, taxi drivers, and politicians of every level including several former presidents. The "At Your Service" guest list reads like a living history of America.

Jim Butler remembers that there were hours where there was no interest at all, where the guests turned out to be "duds."[76] Says Jack Buck about some of those early "At Your Service" programs, "When we did things like Ask the Veterinarian and Ask the Gardener, you would think it was a waste of time, but the telephone lines would light up like Christmas trees. We found when we had Ask the Dentist that there were people who had never been to a dentist in their life. And those subjects helped to educate the listeners in our city. When they tuned in, they knew they were going to learn something.[77]

A call-in format can be difficult for everyone — guests, listeners and hosts alike — however, the KMOX system of eliminating sensationalism but not controversy worked from the very beginning.

Each program was carefully controlled. Guests were informed before they arrived that the broadcast would be approximately forty-five minutes long, with the first ten minutes a conversational interview between the guest and the program host concerning the guest's area of expertise. There would be no script and no prepared text. Next would be a

Bob Hyland looks on as Jack Buck hosts Eleanor Roosevelt on "At Your Service" in 1960. *Hyland Family*

thirty-minute segment of telephone calls from listeners. The guests were asked to answer briefly but completely in order to accommodate as many listeners as possible. In addition, they were told, if necessary, they should feel free to say they didn't know an answer, or suggest another source for an answer or clarification. A guest was asked to observe a few restrictions: no personal attacks on guests or persons not present; no libel,

Jack Buck (left) interviews Marlin Perkins, director of the St. Louis Zoo and popular guest on "At Your Service," in 1964. *Hyland Family*

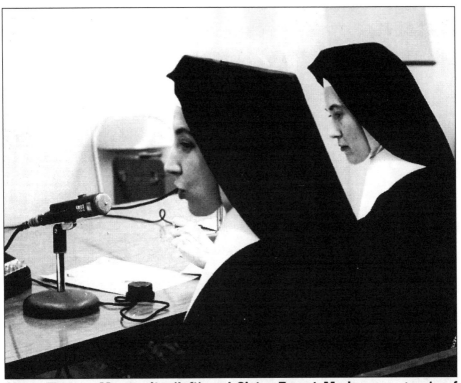

Sister Thomas Marguerite (left) and Sister Ernest Marie were guests of Bob Hardy on "At Your Service" after returning from the Freedom March in Selma, Alabama, in March 1965. *St. Louis Review*

slander or defamation; no profane or obscene language; and no direct advertising of goods or services.[78]

A producer screened each phone call for relevance and appropriateness; however, no calls were censored or rejected. After the call was screened, the caller was allowed on the air. Then the phone was hung up. This prevented a caller from rambling on and backfencing, a two-way conversation between the guest and the caller. As a result, more listeners were able to phone in their questions and the guests could devote more time to answering the questions. KMOX guests didn't always have it easy; sometimes they were put on the spot answering difficult questions, yet they always came back!

Alice Koch English recalls that Hyland,
"always wanted to do things the big way, the best way, the KMOX way," adding *"one of his favorite phrases was 'let's be a*

Father Reinert of St. Louis University joins Hardy in the studio. *Larry Sherron Photography*

radio station.' That meant let's move fast, let's move accurately, and let's bring the people whatever is happening right now."[79]

Thus, the KMOX staff met each morning to plan the day. Consequently, programming flexibility was extremely important. If a significant news story arose, KMOX would be on the air with an expert to discuss it. And if that expert was not in the St. Louis area, long-distance was used. Said Hardy in 1973, "The 'At Your Service' system allows the listener to pose questions in a face-to-face manner while maintaining anonymity, and makes it difficult for the guest to avoid issues. We get the people the audience wants to talk to and give them the opportunity to do so. 'At Your Service' answers the needs of the public."[80]

March 19, 1965 was a perfect example of getting the "right" guests. It was a special "At Your Service" program hosted by Bob Hardy. His guests were two Sisters of Saint Joseph who had joined

From left, St. Louis Mayor Raymond Tucker, Arthur Godfrey and Bob Hardy.
ABK Photo Service

the Selma Freedom March in Selma, Alabama, the previous week. The program, which divided the community, received over 25,000 telephone calls, with 1,000 of those calls coming in long-distance from around the nation. Sister Thomas Marguerite, assistant to the president of Fontbonne College and chairman of its philosophy department, and Sister Ernest Marie, chairman of the college's sociology department, were guests from 3 to 5 in the afternoon. Because of the tremendous response, the two nuns were invited back for two more hours of calls that night with Jack Buck. KMOX estimated that the calls were evenly divided between those in favor of, and those against, the Sisters' actions.

Answering the needs of the public was something KMOX always did well. By 1978, with almost 35,000 experts and nine million listener calls, Robert Hyland had successfully redefined radio as not just something you listen to but rather something that is a part of the community — something that makes a difference. Over the years, the station's information

Hardy and the KMOX 'copter on the roof of the studios on Hampton Avenue.
Hardy Family Archives

programming often made a difference. Here are just a few examples:

A drug addict called in to "At Your Service" guest Don Mitchell, executive director of the Narcotics Service Council. Mitchell made an appointment with the caller and left the program early to meet him. Later, Mitchell reported that the addict was in rehab.

"At Your Service" hosts reported numerous instances of suicide prevention as a result of troubled people calling in and talking to the guest experts. The professionals would work with the callers on the air to prevent them from taking their own lives.

Bob Hardy hosted "At Your Service" from an airplane, commenting on the race from Chicago to St. Louis between a commercial airliner and a STOL (short take-off and landing) plane.

The KMOX traffic helicopter was used to broadcast the only "play-by-play" of the hijacking of a commercial airliner in St. Louis, getting to within fifty feet of the hijacked plane.

With no advance publicity, an "At Your Service" program received 10,000 phone calls for advice on venereal disease.

The county prosecutor, as a KMOX guest, received a call from a man who had to take time off work without pay to appear in court for a traffic violation. After repeated court appearances, the case was still not settled. "At Your Service" and KMOX worked with authorities, and legislation was passed to ensure future cases would be dropped if not prosecuted within two appearances.

After three students were critically injured at a railroad crossing behind Belleville Township High School West, listeners' calls to "At Your Service" resulted in the installation of a crossing signal.

KMOX spearheaded a campaign, through the "At Your Service" program, on behalf of stricter air pollution controls in both the St. Louis area and throughout urban America. The campaign resulted in a full-scale Senate investigation, headed by Senator Edmund Muskie, on the pollution problem in St. Louis. Bob Hardy testified at the subcommittee meeting, turning over a list of eight hundred people who had expressed their concern about the pollution problem.

KMOX Highlights

Anyone ever associated with "The Voice of St. Louis" can name many highlights over the years, and selecting just a few is a difficult task. Since the beginning of "At Your Service" in 1960, the number of important events covered by KMOX is impressive. A few of those highlights, many of which involved Bob Hardy either directly or indirectly, follow.

Documentaries have always played an important role in KMOX programming. In the early years, these in-depth news stories usually lasted from thirty to sixty minutes and aired in full. Later, to keep the audience's attention, the programs were aired in much shorter segments of three to five minutes over the course of several days. Written and produced by the KMOX public affairs and news departments, the station received numerous awards for its work on such subjects as juvenile delinquency, poverty in St. Louis, narcotics addiction, and the lead poisoning contamination of children from paint. The station received the Gavel Award in 1976 from the American Broadcasting Association for the station's campaign against crime, a certificate of merit for a series on the small claims court system, and a Peabody Award for a story on dioxin and Times Beach in the '80s.

The assassination of President John F. Kennedy marked a high point in KMOX history. When the news came across the wire that the president had been shot, several employees at the station wanted to go to the network feeds and get their information from the CBS network. But that wasn't Bob Hyland's style. He insisted on total coverage, with Bob Hardy remaining on the air from one o'clock in the afternoon straight through until the following morning. The KMOX news team got all of their own stories, and the greatest compliment for Hyland and his staff was that by early evening, CBS was picking up stories originating from KMOX.

Bob Hardy personally interviewed every president since Lyndon B. Johnson, an honor he was particularly proud of.

The station made history in 1963 by broadcasting from the floor of the Missouri House of Legislature. Such a broadcast had never been done before, and it was the first of many. In 1965, Bob Hardy served as moderator of the broadcast of the opening session of the Legislature in Jefferson City. The opening address of the Speaker of the House and the Governor's address were included in the broadcast. "The

Doug Newman and Hardy in 1964. *Hardy Family Archives*

Mayor's Town Meetings," a combination of "At Your Service" and town meetings, allowed listeners to phone in and question then Mayor A.J. Cervantes of St. Louis and his Cabinet.

Jack Buck, serving as the master of ceremonies at a variety show, performed for prisoners at Menard Prison and conducted an impromptu interview with six of the inmates. The live broadcast gave St. Louisans a chance to speak to the men, who were serving sentences ranging from two to 199 years for almost every major crime.

October 28, 1965, was a big day for the city of St. Louis. It was the "Topping Out" day, when the center section was placed into the Gateway Arch. KMOX was on hand for a step-by-step description of the proceedings, which marked

On February 24, 1965, from the balcony of the Missouri House of Representatives, Hardy served as commentator for the live broadcast of a debate on the bill to abolish capital punishment. *Wright Studios*

the completion of the outside construction of the monument. Bob Hardy and Jim Butler had done several broadcasts during construction, conducting their programs from a platform on the outside of the north leg of the Arch. For the first broadcasts, Hardy and Butler climbed an outside ladder to the platform. As the Arch grew higher and started its turn inward, the two men rode a creeper crawler up the outside of the leg to a steel ladder surrounded by a circular fence. They would climb the last distance to the platform from which the broadcasts were done. Up until the broadcast at 500 feet, microphone cable and telephone line were used. At 500 feet, they used a new type of microphone — a wireless mike. At the very top, Hardy went out through the hatch once to do a small bit of the broadcast. Hardy called the day the keystone section was set into place, "broadcasting at its best; a true play-by-play broadcast."[81]

Broadcasting from an open platform halfway up the north leg of the Arch, during its construction in 1965. Notice the wireless microphone used by Hardy. *Hardy Family Archives*

KMOX played an important role in another historic day for the city in May 1966: Opening Day for the new Busch Stadium. On the air in 1992, Bob Hardy recalled that day.

"I can remember being assigned to that little rinky-dink Bell helicopter that we started our traffic reports with. It was about six feet long, I think, and it had a bubble on it that looked like a coffee pot. It was really small. And Mr. Hyland wanted to make a big deal out of going from the old stadium to the new stadium, and he wanted me to go in (to Sportsman's Park) with a pilot and pick up home plate, in front of the crowd, then fly out of Sportsman's Park, and go park at Eighteenth Street up on top of the building. Then, two-and-a-half hours later, I was to bring the old home plate into the new stadium. It was a very hot day, and we couldn't get enough lift to get out of Sportsman's Park. We had to make three trips around the field to gain enough speed to get enough altitude to clear the back fence. We finally got out of there. The pilot and I

The view from the broadcast platform, looking south. *Hardy Family Archives*

were both a little shook. We landed down here at the Eighteenth Street garage up on top, it's hotter than bejeebers, and we sat for two hours. Finally, at the prescribed time, we took off…. Can you imagine what it must feel like and look like to fly into the throat of Busch Stadium? I have flown many airplanes in many places, but that day I really had a problem. But anyway, we got the home plate there and everything was fine."[82]

Another event that turned out fine was when Hardy decided to parachute jump and record his thoughts for a program as he floated down to earth. He told Rex Davis of his plans one morning on the air, and said he would play the tapes the following Monday. On Saturday morning, he worked for four hours with members of the St. Louis Parachute Club. They taught him all the techniques he needed to know. He jumped, described the scene and sensation, and landed just as he had been taught earlier in the morning. However, when he played back the tape, it was blank. The

Jim Butler enjoying the view during an Arch broadcast. *Hardy Family Archives*

battery had been jarred loose when he jumped. He decided he would have to jump again or lose his credibility on Monday morning. Parachute club members told him he was probably the only person to ever make a first and second jump in the same day. Hardy protected the recorder on the second jump and got his taped reactions. However, he landed wrong, and although nothing was broken, he had aches and sprains for weeks!

Thousands of pieces of mail came into KMOX when Bob Hardy and Rex Davis solicited rhymes and puns from listeners. The "Dime Rhyme," and "Pun of the Day," were aired on the morning show.

"The Trading Station" turned into a huge hit that continues to this day. The program, originally hosted by Jim Butler, began in 1966. It was an electronic classified ad, enabling

With Walter Burke of McDonnell Aircraft Corporation in 1965, in front of the *Gemini 6* spacecraft. *McDonnell Douglas Corp.*

people to phone in any items they wanted to sell, swap, trade or buy.

Another program that had its debut that year was "Snow Watch," created by Rex Davis. He recalls,

"I created a monster because it got so big. It was very hard to handle. In fact, one morning we closed 132 schools, two of which shouldn't have been, but you'd get mixed-up. The schools had a code word, and when the kids called to try to close their school and

Old Newsboy's Day 1967. From left, Jack Buck, Taffy Wilbur, Jim Butler and Skip Caray. *St. Louis Mercantile Library Association*

Transferring home plate from Sportsman's Park during the opening of Busch Stadium in May 1966. *Hardy Family Archives*

we'd ask for the code word, they'd just hang up. It was a nightmare, but it was a big service and now everyone does it."[83]

KMOX started airing traffic reports for the St. Louis area, and a few weeks later, Don Miller was on another station doing the same thing. Bob Hyland, always looking for the best, didn't waste any time in hiring Miller for KMOX.

The station moved downtown after the city was modernized in the late '60s. In July 1968, the station relocated to new studios in the Gateway Tower. Located in the shadow of the Arch and only a block away from Busch Stadium, the move gave KMOX the most modern, up-to-date radio facilities in the nation. According to Bob Hyland, the move was in keeping with the station's total commitment to the future of the city.

In October 1971, Bob Hardy, at the invitation of Governor Warren E. Hearnes, represented KMOX Radio and Missouri journalists on a trip to the Soviet Union. Eight governors, accompanied by eleven journalists of their own choosing, went for a

Hardy with Missouri Governor Warren E. Hearnes in 1968. *Hardy Family Archives*

two-week trip to the communist country. Upon his return, Hardy had the opportunity to share his experiences behind the Iron Curtain with his listeners in St. Louis.

The political arena has provided many special broadcast moments for KMOX. The station's election coverage has always been superb, as has coverage of the national conventions. Bob Hardy served as anchor at the conventions, doing the "At Your Service" programs, while other KMOX reporters would cover the Missouri and Illinois delegations. The total coverage was always exceptional. One convention in particular — the Democratic National Convention in Miami Beach in July 1972 — stands out for many St. Louisans. The Democratic presidential nominee, George McGovern, had indicated to Senator Thomas Eagleton that he (Eagleton) was

With the Missouri and Illinois Caucus at the 1968 Democratic Convention. From left, Hardy, Warren Hearnes and Pat O'Brien. Background upper left, Melvin Price and Jim Symington. *Barlow Photography*

A popular format for KMOX advertising, featuring the on-air personalities from 1969. *KMOX*

McGovern's choice for vice president. Bob Hardy, covering the convention for KMOX, knew Eagleton well from having him on "At Your Service" many times. Hardy, thinking it would be a great news story, asked Eagleton for permission to camp out in Eagleton's room so he could be there when the call came through from McGovern. Eagleton agreed, so Hardy was in the room while other reporters waited outside.

Lucy Ann Boston, "Life Style" reporter and former Globe-Democrat *reporter recalled, "I was one of the reporters standing outside Room 605 [when Senator Eagleton was named George McGovern's vice presidential running mate and was to get the call in his hotel room in Florida at the political convention] ... and somebody said they opened the door.... 'Oh, Hardy's in there, okay'... any of us would have given our eye teeth to be in that room.... But if we couldn't be in there, I don't think there's any-body that any of us trusted more to be in there than Bob Hardy. He was so fair and so accurate and such a sharing colleague, that we knew he would obviously get the news back to KMOX right away ... but as soon as he came out, he would tell us everything. He would not withhold anything, and we would get our stories, too."*[84]

The call came, Eagleton accepted the nomination, and Hardy reported back to KMOX on the Jack Carney show. Hardy had the only tape of the conversation between McGovern and Eagleton, which would later come to play an important role in the events that followed. Eagleton was later dropped from the ticket because of his alleged answers to questions pertaining to his medical treatment. Hardy's tape of Eagleton's side of the conversation helped set the record straight as to the questions asked of Eagleton and his answers.

KMOX won many awards in its history, particularly after the programming change to news and information. One of the most prestigious came in 1974 when the station received the 40th National Headliner Award for Outstanding Public Service by a Radio Station. The award was presented for KMOX's campaign to open the sessions of the Missouri State

Senate to the broadcast media the previous year. Bob Hardy, director of Public Affairs and Special Events at the time, accepted the honor for the station.

As "The Voice of St. Louis" celebrated its 50th anniversary, Bob Hyland decided to give the community a birthday gift. He created "Call for Action," the first program of its kind in St. Louis. A confidential service, its purpose was to help people solve problems they couldn't solve on their own. It turned out to be a welcome addition to the KMOX services — over 10,000 people used the service the first year.

A high point in the station's programming each year was "Washington Week," when Hardy would go to Washington, D.C., and conduct live interviews with Cabinet members, department heads, various senators, and other political newsmakers in the nation's capital.

Celebrating the "At Your Service" format's tenth anniversary, Bob Hyland joins Bob Hardy on the air. *KMOX*

The addition of Jack Carney to the KMOX staff cannot be overlooked, as Carney himself became one of the station's notable highlights. Carney came to KMOX in the early '70s from San Francisco, although earlier in his career, he had been in St. Louis at WIL. According to Jim Butler, Carney gave KMOX, a station that was primarily devoted to news and sports, a whole different element of fun and entertainment. Bob Costas likened Carney's role at "The Voice of St. Louis" to that of "the guy making mischief in the palace."[85] Carney was always doing something a little bit different.

Costas also remembers Carney's originality. "Carney started doing these radio skits that he would star in as Tiki Jack. They were absurd parodies of radio soap operas and he was this guy, Tiki Jack … traveling the world, enforcing justice, and I was his callow assistant, Rob Roy. He would write these scripts, and they were very funny, with sound effects and everything. And then he would bring people in, famous people who were in town or noted local personalities, to play a cameo role."[86]

Carney had quite a following, and some thought he was even better than Arthur Godfrey. He knew how to entertain the KMOX audience in a way that has not been matched.

October 1975 stands out in KMOX history. Until that time, "The Voice of St. Louis" had not had a

Jack Carney. *KMOX*

consistent, strong, female presence on the air. The hiring of Anne Keefe changed all that. Keefe had worked in television in Rochester, New York, but fit right in to Bob Hyland's "At Your Service" programming.

In 1981, Hardy became, in his own words, "a U.S. correspondent of sorts for 4GG," a radio station serving the Gold Coast of Australia. His daily feed was done via telephone and satellite. "American Newsline" came about after Australian radio executives toured KMOX to decide if they wanted to copy the KMOX format. The program reached finalist status in the International Radio Festival Awards in 1983.

KMOX was in Berlin the day the wall came down in November

Jack Carney's 9 a.m. to noon show provided every-thing from laughs to serious information. *T. Mike Fletcher*

1989. Kevin McCarthy, who at the time did the afternoon show on KLOU (KMOX's FM station) and regularly filled in on KMOX, received a "tip" from a colleague in Berlin. McCarthy, who had just gone on the air, received permission from Hyland to go to Berlin and cover the events for "The Voice of St. Louis."

C-Span chose Bob Hardy as one of seven talk-show personalities featured during a week of talk-radio broadcasts. The public affairs network televised live from the KMOX

An ad from 1978. *KMOX*

radio studios on May 31, 1990, as Hardy hosted a program simulcast with Moscow Radio.

One of KMOX's most memorable highlights was the establishment of a "radio bridge" linking former enemies. With the advent of Mikhail Gorbachev's *glasnost* and *perestroika* policy in the late '80s, Hyland took advantage of the new openness to start a special series of regularly scheduled broadcasts between the people of Moscow and the people of St. Louis. Hyland had heard an experimental broadcast where several stations were to speak with Moscow, but felt it wasn't done very well. He believed that with the "At Your Service" experience of his staff, KMOX could do a global program of much better quality. He pursued the idea, making it clear that the program must have open conversation and no censorship. Moscow Radio agreed, and the program became very successful. Said Hardy in 1992,

"And that's when the radio listeners of KMOX met Sergei Goryachov for the first time ... himself a young broadcaster, a radio producer for Moscow Radio ... now having climbed the

Traffic reporter Don Miller and KMOX Copter One. *Fostaire Helicopters and Don Miller*

ladder even further ... a young man with his own television show and an audience of seven million people."[87]

The program enabled listeners in both countries to speak with, and learn from, one another. Kevin McCarthy believes,

"St. Louis was treated to a very unique insight to Russian life with Muscovites on the air, with everything from school children and their teachers to the conductor of the Symphony and the mayors of their cities."[88]

Jeanette Hoag Grider believes this series was one of the highlights of Bob Hardy's career.

"Nothing was more exciting to Bob than the start of our year-long series of special programs with Sergei in Moscow. The monthly hour-long broadcasts were anchored by Bob and a host at Radio Moscow ... and featured topics that went beyond news and

Bill Wilkerson, Wendy Wiese and Bob Hardy had the top rated morning show in the market, and consistently ranked in the top five in the nation.
Larry Sherron Photography

politics to the daily lives of American and Soviet citizens. It was a great opportunity to compare the similarities families and individuals share in both countries. It was wonderful to have Soviet moms talking about the challenges of communicating with their teens, and teens talking about their tastes in music and clothes."[89]

Although it was a challenge for everyone involved, the series was a great success. It brought the people of two cities — half a world apart and with distinctly different philosophies — closer together.

The series also brought about another major highlight in KMOX's history and Bob Hardy's career. As Hardy explained on the air in 1992,

THE NEWSMEN

4GG NEWS. . .LOCAL STATE NATIONAL AND INTERNATIONAL NEWS

Radio 120

The Gold Coasts Own Radio Station

Hardy's daily feed to Australia brought American news to listeners of 4GG Radio on the Gold Coast.
4GG and Gold Coast Bulletin

"Sergei said after about a year and a half into this series, 'Why don't you come to Moscow and do a live broadcast from Red Square?'... and we said that would be a great idea. So we approached Mr. Hyland with the idea and he said, 'Wait a minute, let me get this right. You want to take a crew from KMOX and spend all that money to *go over and do one, one-hour show in Moscow?' We thought it was a rather impressive thing to do. But he wanted to think about it. He did for about a half a day and he called us in and said, 'Here's what we'll do. We will do five cities in five countries in five days, and you will broadcast one hour of live "At Your Service" with guests, back through satellite to our KMOX listeners. And you will wrap up those five cities in five countries in five consecutive days with a broadcast in Moscow.' We told him it was impossible, and Mr. Hyland used one of his favorite lines, 'Nothing is impossible if you don't have to do it yourself.' In other words — go team, and get it done."[90]*

The special series took tremendous planning and coordination, but culminated in live broadcasts, using the "At Your Service" format, from Berlin, Prague, Budapest, Warsaw and Moscow's Red Square. In charge of the project was KMOX's manager of operations, Kevin Young. Bob Hardy and Kevin McCarthy would serve as hosts on the programs. Peggy Cohill Drenkhahn, executive producer of "At Your Service," arranged the special guests in each city. Paul Grundhauser,

During a presidential visit to St. Louis in February 1983, Hardy directs questions from the audience to President Reagan. *Hardy Family Archives*

the station's chief engineer, took care of all equipment and technical arrangements. McCarthy's wife, Gudrun, who is German, served as interpreter. Also traveling were Hardy's wife, Re, and Grundhauser's wife, Michelle. A completely equipped motor coach, used by President Bush on an earlier trip to Europe, would be the home of the KMOX team for the week.

The Berlin broadcast originated from Radio in the American Sector (RIAS), and took the form of a town hall meeting. Equally divided between East and West Berliners, a total of fifty Germans discussed honestly and candidly their problems since the wall had come down.

Czech Radio was the source for the Prague broadcast. Paul Grundhauser had to rewire everything to get hooked up to the satellite dish, as the wiring was about forty years old. One of the show's guests was Ambassador Shirley Temple Black.

Hardy interviews First Lady Barbara Bush in 1985. *Hardy Family Archives*

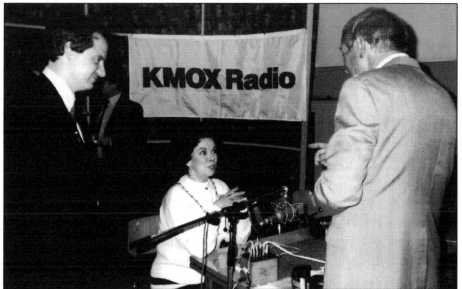

In Prague, with Ambassador Shirley Temple Black.

At Radio in the American Sector (RIAS). Kneeling, Paul Grundhauser, KMOX Chief Engineer, from left, Michelle Bagatti; Boris Ivashkov, of Omni Venturecapital; Re Hardy; Bob Hardy; Kevin Young, KMOX manager of operations; Gudrun McCarthy; Kevin McCarthy; Rik DeLisle of RIAS, and Jo Eager DeLisle.

Pages 115-116: Highlights of the Eastern European trip. *Paul Grundhauser and Hardy Family Archives*

Conducting the live broadcast from Red Square.

Hardy and Tatiana Zeleranskaya interviewing a young man during the live broadcast from Red Square.

In Budapest, Radio Bridge, a part of Voice of America, was to be the site for the broadcast. Since the entire facility consisted of two small offices, the decision was made to turn the small conference room aboard the motor coach into a broadcast studio. Two guests on the show were recently appointed ministers in the new Hungarian government.

The Warsaw broadcast originated from the CBS News Bureau. The guests included two journalists, one from a daily newspaper and the other from a Catholic weekly.

The broadcast from Red Square on April 28, 1990, was done with the help of Sergei Goryachov, Tatiana Zeleranskaya, and Moscow Radio. As the KMOX team set up the equipment on Red Square, about 15,000 troops were massing to practice for the upcoming May Day celebration and parade. The troops waited for the finish of the broadcast, but the broadcast team had to leave Red Square immediately following the radio program. During the live broadcast, the crowd grew to about three hundred, with many of them asking questions to the listeners back in St. Louis.

The special series of broadcasts from Eastern Europe was a

Hardy and wife, Re, in Berlin. *Hardy Family Archives*

milestone in the station's history, and earned Bob Hardy and KMOX Radio its second National Headliner Award.

Hardy's reputation as a newsman and his association with the U.S. Air Force, resulted in another outstanding achievement for him and KMOX. In December 1990, U.S. troops moved into the Persian Gulf and Desert Shield became daily news. Hardy suggested that he and a crew from "The Voice of St. Louis" travel to Saudi Arabia to bring live broadcasts back to St. Louis listeners. In addition, he would do "At Your Service"-type programs with troops from the metropolitan area who were stationed in Saudi Arabia. This would allow the troops the opportunity to "talk" to their families and friends back home.

At Red Square in Moscow. From left, Kevin Young, Tatiana Zeleranskaya, Paul Grundhauser, Bob Hardy and Sergei Goryachov.

A live broadcast from the previously closed border, shortly after the Berlin Wall came down.

On December 8, 1990, Hardy, Kevin McCarthy, and Paul Grundhauser of KMOX, along with Larry Conners, John Martin, and Scott Thomas of KMOV-TV, left Dover Air Force Base in Delaware, on a C-5 Galaxy, the largest cargo airplane in the free world. The group had received special clearance from the Department of the Air Force to travel via Military Airlift Command aircraft to and from the Persian Gulf. The airplane was loaded with military personnel and equipment destined for Desert Shield.

The first leg of the trip, from Dover to Torrejon Air Base near Madrid, Spain, stood out for Hardy. Hardy had been a private pilot and had taken his son-in-law, Glen Chinn, an Air Force pilot, flying on many occasions. This flight was special to Glen because he was finally able to take his father-in-law flying. He was on the crew, and flew the C-5 to Spain.

Hardy's son-in-law, Major Glen Chinn, piloted the C-5 Galaxy that carried Paul Grundhauser, Kevin McCarthy and Hardy on the first leg of their trip to Saudi Arabia during Desert Shield in December 1990. *Hardy Family Archives*

With visas good for forty-eight hours, the KMOX team hit the sand running, and spent most of their time conducting interviews and broadcasting back to St. Louis. The trip was extremely successful, and received compliments from civilians and military personnel alike. Home again, Hardy received a letter from a longtime KMOX listener who had been included in one of the live broadcasts. Air Force Lieutenant Stephen Knight thanked Hardy for the opportunity to take part in the program, and noted that some of his superior officers had been concerned about the live broadcast. He wrote,

"You'll be glad to know that, as we drove back to our quarters after the program, the public affairs officer was extremely satisfied with the whole experience, and considered it a rare, positive encounter with the media. We all felt we'd been given a chance to speak freely, without fear of being manipulated. He commented

Sergei Goryachov and Hardy in the KMOX studio in September 1991. *Hardy Family Archives*

that he would be more secure the next time around because of the treatment received by you and your staff. I congratulate you and KMOX for your responsible style of journalism. You definitely reflected positively on the St. Louis community in a sincere attempt to serve public interest."[91]

The Sports Voice
of St. Louis

It is impossible to talk about KMOX without talking about sports. Sports have always played an important part in the broadcast day at "The Voice of St. Louis," and the station has taken great pride in its reputation as one of the nation's greatest sports stations.

Not long after the creation of "At Your Service" on KMOX, Bob Hyland wanted to extend the format to sports. The Sports Open Line has now been on the air for more than thirty-five years, the longest running sports talk program on radio. Some of the biggest names in the sports world have been guests on the show, including Stan Musial, Yogi Berra, Willie Mays, Don Shula, Ozzie Smith, Jerry Rice, Tommy Lasorda, Brett Hull and Wayne Gretzky. "Sports on a Sunday Morning" was another Hyland creation, and one that remains unique in broadcasting.

KMOX has always broadcast sports events, even in its early years. But, as in other aspects of the station, Bob Hyland made KMOX and sports broadcasts synonymous, calling the station "The Sports Voice of St. Louis." Hyland also made Cardinal baseball the centerpiece of that identity.

Hyland, having grown up in St. Louis, understood that his hometown was a sports town, especially a baseball town. He knew that radio coverage of the Cardinals would give the station a vast audience throughout the Midwest, and if

KMOX had the exclusive rights to Cardinal baseball broadcasts, then the audience would always turn to 1120 on the radio dial.

As Bob Costas explains, "If you own the rights to the Cardinals, other stations can talk about the Cardinals but no one else can have those games, and you can't counter the Cardinals with anything."[92]

Hence, the Cardinal Baseball Network, operated by "The Voice of St. Louis," started in March of 1965 with 100 stations in 10 states. By 1978, it was the nation's largest sports network with 115 stations in 11 states. Coverage of the Cardinals has always included broadcasts of all regular season games, spring training games, post-season Cardinal games, as well as pre-game and post-game shows and interviews.

The importance Hyland placed on sports was clear when

From left, Dan Dierdorf, Bob Costas, Harry Caray and Bill Wilkerson decide which is tastier, a Chicago hot dog or a St. Louis hot dog, for the Friday Frank Forecast, a weekly ritual between Costas and Dierdorf in 1985. *Jim Herren Photography*

KMOX became the first commercial station to broadcast a complete baseball game from Japan, with the Cardinals playing there in 1958. In 1976, the station added another first with a live broadcast of the National Football League, with Jack Buck, Dan Kelly and Bill Wilkerson providing all the action coverage at the exhibition game between the Big Red and the San Diego Chargers in Tokyo, Japan.

The magnitude of KMOX's sports coverage was remarkable. In the early '80s, KMOX was the only major radio station broadcasting up to 350 sporting events live every year, equaling a full quarter of its programming. Not only was Cardinal baseball on the air, but Hyland made it a point to include all sports action: Blues hockey, Cardinal football, Saint Louis University Billikens basketball, University of Missouri basketball and football, and professional basketball – originally the Hawks, then the Spirits, when they were a presence in St. Louis. It's been said that KMOX at one time had the rights to

The voices of the Cardinals, Jack Buck and Mike Shannon. *KMOX*

every sport in the city. It also has been said that Hyland may not have cared that much about some sports, but KMOX carried them if only so no one else could. Jack Buck recalls, "It took some scheduling to get all the sports on the air sometimes because the games and schedules overlapped."[93]

KMOX's reputation as a sports station grew over the years, and the community knew where to go for the big sports stories. Bob Costas says,

"If Lou Brock would have gotten traded, everybody in St. Louis would immediately push the button to KMOX even if they hadn't been listening to it in the first place. It's possible that if a big news story developed, you might turn on the television set or you might go to another radio station. But it was unthinkable if it was something in sports to be anywhere other than KMOX. We just didn't have the sports, we had the person who was regarded as the best at that particular sport whatever it was."[94]

And some of the best and most important names in sports broadcasting got their start at KMOX. The list is impressive — Bob Costas, Jack Buck, Harry Caray, Dan Dierdorf, Dan Kelly, Joe Garagiola, Bob Starr, and Bill White, who went on to become the president of the National League in baseball — to name just a few.

The extent to which KMOX covered sports was not equaled at other CBS radio stations, which often avoided heavy play-by-play commitments. But it remains clear to millions of listening sports fans, that KMOX's coverage of sports is a major reason the station consistently ranks number one.

KMOX Late Night

For more than twenty years, KMOX has had one of the most successful late night programs in radio with Jim White. Also known to his listeners as "the Big Bumper," White hosts a nighttime version of "At Your Service." White has a following that most in the industry would envy. But late night at KMOX has always had a great following, since that's when "The Voice of St. Louis" becomes the voice that reaches so much farther.

In the early '50s, Jim Butler was the host for a late night program called the "All Night Frolic"; the same type of broadcast being heard on most radio stations in the country. KMOX, however, added something unique to only three other stations in North America.

Butler recalls airing two-and-a-half minute hard-sell commercials referred to as P.I.'s, or "per inquiries," from 11:30 p.m. to about 5 a.m. These can be compared to today's infomercials. The purpose of a P.I. was to sell an item by mail, with the listener sending a check or money order to KMOX for the item. Tomato plants; elastic socks, one size fits all; and, plastic tablecloths with a picture of the Last Supper or the Lord's Prayer, were just a few of the more bizarre items for sale. A station in Cincinnati was the only other station broadcasting P.I.'s in the U.S., but there were two 50,000-watt stations broadcasting from Mexico, right on the Texas border.[95]

The musical theme of late night continued into the late '50s, albeit with a different host, or shall we say, hostess. Lou Payne was known as "the lady in the dark" with the sultry voice. She averaged more than 100 calls per night with song requests.

Probably the best known KMOX late night music show host was "the man who walks and talks at midnight," John McCormick. His distinctive, deep, mellow, soothing voice was perfect for late night/early morning radio music programming. And his huge listening audience most likely never knew some of his endearing indiosyncrasies.

Rich Dalton remembers his intern days at KMOX. "I was an intern from SIUE and worked at KMOX in '70 or '71. I was Jim White's assistant, and later wrote news for John McCormick. John McCormick was pretty cool. He was smooth as silk. He was dapper and distinguished. He had been a pilot in World War II, drove a Corvette customized by Andy Granatelli, and had done a TV show

Lou Payne, KMOX's nighttime disc jockey in the late '50s. *St. Louis Mercantile Library Association*

in Chicago among other things. He would descend from the upstairs office with a box. In it was his stuff, mail, copy, Camels, a sensor light, and a piece of black cloth. He used one of the smaller studios, the one used by the staff announcers (Doug Newman, Jack Warnick, and Jim Butler) during the day. He plugged in the tiny desk light, turned off the studio lights so that it was otherwise dark. He spread out the black cloth and opened up the pack of Camels. He took about ten or so out of the pack and lined them up side by side on the cloth. He arranged his ashtray, copy, letters and other stuff just so. Then when the midnight news was over, he was on! 'The man who walks and talks' also ate **White Castles**! He would give me money and I would drive over to the White Castle that used to be on Chouteau Avenue. I wish I could remember how many he would order for himself. He would sit in his darkened corner studio and play Frank Sinatra to half of the United States and eat belly bombers!"[96]

"The Voice of St. Louis" hit upon a winning combination when Robert Hyland made the decision to do talk radio at night, followed by John McCormick. KMOX was number one in the ratings except at night, when other stations were grabbing the available audience with the Top 40s and rock 'n' roll. The station was airing Harry Fender from the Steeplechase Room, which had a large audience, but not as large as Hyland wanted. He decided to try talk and put Jim White on as host. As soon as the station went to the talk format in this time slot, the ratings jumped to first place. White enjoyed the night hours, but not when it was combined with morning drive and afternoons. He remembers finally telling Hyland he would do day or night but not both, and that his preference was night.

"Nights being to Hyland 4 to 6 in the afternoon and 8 to midnight, I finally quit the afternoon drive and stretched the night show from 9 p.m. to 3 a.m.; then from 10 p.m. to 2 a.m., where it's been for a number of years."[97]

After some experimenting, an Open Line format was found to be the most appealing to the audience and to the station. The audience loved the nighttime talk, a relatively new concept around the country, and the station no longer had to find guests for the show, who had proved unwilling to come into the studio late at night.

One guest that didn't mind being on late at night was David Hoy. Rich Dalton recalls nights when Hoy was White's guest. "David was a psychic. People went crazy when he was on! I would sit with the producer (Marino Garcia) and help out. The phone had about fifteen or so lines as I recall. There was an odometer-like device hooked to the phone cable to count over-calls (calls that didn't get through because the lines were all busy). Usually there weren't many over-calls, but when you had a hot topic the counter would click and count up maybe fifty or sixty in an hour. When David Hoy was on, the counter would click continuously. He would have hundreds of over-calls! He could be pretty amazing at times. I remember him telling someone where to find her lost wedding ring. He said it was in the lining of a steamer trunk that she had cleaned up a month earlier. I heard her come back to the phone after she ran upstairs to her attic. She was breathless but ecstatic. It was right where he said it would be!"[98]

White's show was a family affair for a time.

"My wife [Pat] booked guests for the show for a while. She worked out of the house and used her maiden name so it wouldn't sound hokey. Her 'Executive Producer' sign is still hanging on the door of the office at home. She was even on the air with me for a short period of time." [99]

Topics for White's show vary. He usually goes into the studio with three or four topics that are very broad in scope. However, it's typical that someone will call about something totally different and by the end of the night, the topics have changed completely. He says that it's not unusual to have half a dozen general topics going at any given time. One thing special about his program, he says, is that "if we're talking about something specific that happened somewhere, sometimes we'll get a call from that specific place. Then my listeners can get the thoughts from the folks where an event actually took place."[100]

White believes the reason his program has lasted so long and has been so popular is because of his philosophy for the night show. "I call it the 4-F Club — Forum for Functional Folks. I really believe

*that most people out there are normal. Some of the best shows we do are situations where anybody can put themselves into, not the sort of topics you find on daytime television, but real dilemma situations....
I don't cater to night people — the program is a day program at nighttime. Sometimes people say I shouldn't yell because I wake them up and I say, 'If you're trying to sleep, don't listen to me, turn on some classical music.' But I try to relate one-on-one to normal people. I think at nighttime we have a better chance for a real cross-section of public opinion, so I aim it to the normal rather than the abnormal. If you go out to shock the people, then you have to keep going one step further to continue shocking them, and finally you go so far, you fall off the edge — either you get so outrageous you get fired or sued or arrested or punched in the mouth, and then your career is over. So it's*
better to stay main-stream!"[101]

White realizes that part of his job is to hang up on callers. He has no qualms about doing it, and he sometimes takes heat from listeners. But as he explains, "If a caller is boring, I have a very short period of time to do something about it or I'm going to lose my audience."[102]

Over the years, White's audience has continued to grow. The pro-

KMOX's "Big Bumper," Jim White. *KMOX*

gram averages 5,000 calls per night, with as many as 30,000 calls on one subject. Calls come in from all over the world, the farthest one, for White, coming from Guam. White, who has heard from listeners in Guatemala, Finland, Canada, and every state in the country, says, "That's one reason I really enjoy nights, because when you pick up the phone, you never know where the call is coming from!"[103]

Souvenirs
of Days Gone By

As I spoke to people about their KMOX experiences, they remembered the station and how it had such an impact on their lives. In addition, as others heard of this project, I received many letters with special remembrances.

We begin with one of Bob Hardy's comments during the tribute to Robert Hyland in 1992.

"He had a sense of humor and you could have fun with him. But, you know, there was an interesting side to Bob Hyland that not too many people recognize. He played jokes on his department heads, but he rarely played jokes on his 'on-the-air' people. He was so serious about what went on the air here, that he would never put himself in a position of getting somebody off the straight and narrow by virtue of a gag or a joke. He just didn't think that it was the place to play fun and games on a live mike."[104]

Jack Buck recalled a memorable conversation with Bob Hyland.

"I was on the phone with him, speaking from Los Angeles ... and on the thirtieth floor of the hotel. The conversation was almost concluded, and I said, 'Bob, hang on a minute, the chandelier is starting to swing. We're having an earthquake here!' He said, 'Really? Hold on and I'll put you on the air with Jack Carney.' I said, 'Baloney! You want me to hang on and I'm thirty floors high in the middle of an earthquake?' I think that's the only time I ever hung up on him before he hung up on me."[105]

Bob Costas recollects his first day at KMOX.

"The first day that I was there, Jack Buck brought me in to 'At Your Service' and Jim White was hosting. During the break, I went out to get a cup of coffee from the machine, and I remember Jim White saying, 'That's verboten. *You're not allowed to have any coffee or anything in the studio.' And that struck me as the weirdest thing. But in a way, the message that those little peculiar things sent was important not for the specific rule but for the tone that it set ... that there was a sanctity about KMOX, and that it was different from other places."[106]*

Jack Buck recalled the beginning of "At Your Service,"

"Hyland gave away the majority of the record library so no one would be tempted to go back to music. We still have a couple of thousand records, but we used to have 20,000 or so."[107]

and remembers the night Ken Boyer was traded,

"People had the opportunity to call in, and they blew the phone company off the air. The switchboard was so swamped, the calls couldn't come in."[108]

Kevin McCarthy recalls the respect he was shown when on assignment for KMOX in other countries,

"KMOX was known worldwide as 'America's radio station.'"[109]

John Angelides, news director, says KMOX had an impact on the listeners and the city.

"KMOX has made its listeners a lot smarter and wiser. It has made the quality of life in St. Louis much better. It symbolized what was good about journalism in the community because I always thought it was fair and balanced in the way that it handled various issues. My legacy is that we presented the listeners with fair, balanced, accurate reporting without sensationalizing the misfortunes of others."[110]

Jim White credits Bob Hardy for his move to St. Louis and KMOX.

"Bob was listening to the radio late one night and came across KDKA in Pittsburgh. He called, but I wasn't really wanting to leave. My family was there, it was my hometown.... Bob had Donna Johnson, the secretary for the newsroom, meet me at the airport and we went to breakfast.... She drove me downtown to the studios, and

everything was almost brand new. I had never seen anything like this, a radio station that had been built to be a radio station — it was awesome! I took a tour of the station, met everybody, and sat in the studio during the 'Interfaith Panel' program that was on for years and years. Bob told me he was looking for an assistant news director who would also do special assignments and a couple of newscasts. He said nothing about talk radio at that time. The last item on the agenda was to meet Mr. Hyland who was, as usual, sitting behind his immaculate desk. I smoked at the time and nervously lit up a cigarette. He pushed his Steuben ashtray over and said, 'Well, what's it going to take to get you down here?' and that was it. So I hit him with a salary that I thought was outrageous at the time — turned out later it wasn't — and he said, 'What else?' and I told him that was it. I left his office, hopped in a cab, got to the airport, and called Pat and told her to start packing, we were moving to St. Louis. I went in the next day to KDKA to resign, and the manager was so mad at me he fired me. Then Bob [Hardy] called,

Hardy watches workers make way for the Arch in 1960. *Alfred Fleishman*

and said there were some other problems, and that I shouldn't do anything yet. So I was without a job for two weeks, but it finally worked out, and I came to St. Louis."[111]

White recollects working with Hardy during afternoon drive time. "Hyland put Bob and me on in the afternoon and we became known as 'The Babbling Bookends' — Jack Buck came up with that name. During that time we had Friday afternoon Happy Hour. We told people to go out and do fun things. So we went out one day and flew a kite off the balcony. We brought in a wading pool one day, set it up on the balcony, filled it with fall leaves and jumped in. And one day we had a picnic out there. There was just this sense of playfulness."[112]

Hardy and White also did the morning drive together for a while.

"Something that Bob and I cooked up many years ago on the morning show — the Knobnoster University Marching Band.... I'll tell you how it all came about — I remember it vividly. Bob and I were doing the show. It was April 1, I don't remember what year it was ... and at that time, in addition to his other duties, Jack Carney was in charge of all the music on KMOX because he knew something about music.... He would always send down the morning march on a tape, with no label or anything, and we had a little sheet of paper, 'And now, here's the morning march.' We let fly and there's this horrible ruckus, 'Stars and Stripes Forever,' and Bob and I had tears in our eyes, we were laughing so hard, and after it was over, Bob looked at me and said, 'And what school is that from, Jim?' And I looked down at the desk in front of me and I had the list of weather conditions from across the state and my eye fell on Knobnoster, so it became the Knobnoster University Marching Band, Paul Boomer, director."[113]

Bob Hardy and Rex Davis had fun one April Fools' Day, but listeners and Bob Hyland didn't appreciate the joke, according to one KMOX employee.

"One April Fools' Day, Hardy and Davis played the morning march one hour early, then when it was over, they said, 'April Fools'.' But Mr. Hyland was not amused, and Rex and Bob were in the doghouse for a few days. The phones were said to be ringing off *the hook that morning, and people thought their clocks were wrong and it threw the city into mass confusion. Southwestern Bell told Mr. Hyland that they had never received so many phone calls on their circuits at the same time. This is because so many regular listeners know exactly what they need to be doing or where they need to be in the morning according to what is on the air at that moment."*[114]

KMOX listeners have become comfortable in knowing what to expect. Says an unidentified KMOX employee,

"Richard Evans has been dead for years, and yet the listeners got very upset when KMOX took the 'Thought For The Day' off the air. There was so much input to the station that we put the program back on the air."[115]

An unidentified listener said in 1992,

"I always have three radios on in my house — KMOX takes the

Hardy arriving by helicopter on the scene of a news story in 1966. *Buzz Taylor*

place of television for me."[116]

Charles Brennan, who hosts the "Morning Meeting" at KMOX, recalls his first impressions of Bob Hardy.

"When I arrived in September 1988, I sat in on Bob's show over the noon hour. What struck me about the show was the lack of rancor, and the tremendous amount of rapport between Bob and the guests. It was as if they had all convened around the lunch table to talk about the issues of the day in a gentlemanly and respectful manner. That was the tone he set for the station and for the show, until the day he died. I don't know of many hosts in the country who were ever able to connect so well with his listeners. That's rare in this business."[117]

Mary Ann Hagedorn, a listener, sent her memory of Bob Hardy.

Charles Brennan. *KMOX*

Bob [Hardy] always gave the farm report. Well, this one day, Bill asked what it all meant — beans?, gills? Well, Bob started to explain. Bill and Wendy had no idea what Bob was saying, and they were all laughing while Bob was so serious, and then he couldn't help but get silly, too. I was driving the car, and I had to pull over because I was crying with laughter. To this day, every time I hear the farm report on

KMOX, I remember Bob Hardy with love and admiration.[118]

Wendy Wiese recollects,

*"Mr. Hyland always took great pride in calling Bob Hardy **his** Walter Cronkite."*[119]

Jeanette Hoag Grider was the producer of the morning show with Bob Hardy, Bill Wilkerson and Wendy Wiese.

"When KMOX went to a new combo board system and on-air talent switched to running their own board (instead of having a board operator or engineer), the break-in period was a little tough. In addition to interviewing the guest and taking listener questions, hosts were now responsible for the technical end of their programs (turning on the microphones, running the phone call-in system and initiating commercial carts, as well as playing newscarts in the studio and joining the network at the top of the hour). Everyone struggled to become familiar with a board that looked like the dash of a 747, and the mistakes were frequent and the frustration on-going. During the noon show one day, there had been several problems with carts and the phones. Bob threw it to a break and as the commercial played, he hit the intercom to talk to me and let loose with a stream of expletives about the equipment and what a bunch of 'bull____' it was to deal with. Seeing the red light to indicate a live microphone, I was frantically waving my arms to try to stop Bob and, of course, his live mike muted my side of the intercom. He finally realized what had happened, and ever the gentleman, he came out of the break and apologized to his listeners, explaining his frustration with the equipment."[120]

Grider shared a funny memory of the morning show,

"One morning Bob misread his news copy about a new strain of organisms. It came out 'orgasms,' and Bob had no

Sportscaster Skip Caray and weather announcer Pat Fontaine in 1967. *Jim Miller Jr.*

idea why Bill and Wendy were falling off the chair laughing."[121]

and her memory of Hardy and Hyland,

"Bob Hyland used to call Bob Hardy 'The General,' because of his military background, and because he had a pair of sunglasses that made him look somewhat like General MacArthur. It was a gag between them."[122]

Jill Grimes remembers her first experience with KMOX.

"I was born and raised in southern California and lived there until my second marriage to a St. Louisan in 1988. Both my father and first husband were in the television industry as directors, so media has always been a part of my life and with it, a genuine awareness as to what it included. I was a regular listener of the CBS affiliate in Los Angeles, so it was quite natural for me to wake up to KMOX the first morning in our new home here in St. Louis. Although, what I heard that morning made me sit upright in bed and turn the volume up on the radio, as I had never heard anything remotely like it in all the years in L.A. To my never-ending joy and amazement, at 5:55 in the morning, I heard the singing of the Lord's Prayer. I woke my husband of one week and asked what was happening, was there some kind of special meaning? He laughed at my surprise and said it was a daily occurrence on KMOX. Needless to say, we are still loyal listeners to KMOX."[123]

Cathy Gamble, former KMOX/KLOU controller, points out,

Clarence Nieder, Harry Fender and Bob Gotsch in 1967.

"You have to look at the WIL-KMOX connection. That was the recruiting point for KMOX. We got Hardy, Carney, and Osborne."[124]

And an unidentified listener, in 1993, had fond memories of them.

"Bob Hardy, Jack Carney, and Bob Osborne had to be the

greatest trio that ever lived."[125]

Carol Reigle of Trenton, Illinois, sent this note.

Bob Hardy was family to all of our family — we were early morning listeners forever. I have an autographed note from (Bob Hardy) dated September 28, 1982. Our daughter, Carolyn, worked in the office at Jim's Formal Wear in Trenton. Bob came in for a tux one day and Carolyn asked him to sign a memo sheet for her mom. He kindly wrote this message to me —

September 28, 1982

Hi Carol, Carolyn says you're an early morning listener. Thanks much! Bob Hardy, KMOX.[126]

Bill Wilkerson recalls his first days at KMOX.

"I started as a newswriter without ever writing news. The person who was to train me spent the first night talking about her boyfriend in Missoula, Montana, so I learned nothing. The second night, she didn't show up. McCormick wanted his news and I said, 'I'm in training.' He said to forget that, he wanted the news. So I was going to quit, but decided to stay the night. Hyland called me in the next day, and said he knew the girl didn't show up and that she was fired, so the job was mine."[127]

Wilkerson will never forget his first news assignment.

"My first-ever news assignment was going out to the airport and covering Vice President Spiro Agnew, just because Bob Hardy said I should do it."[128]

In a 1992 letter to Bob Hardy, David Christoff recalled evenings in front of the radio with his grandmother.

In the early 1950s, my grandfather died and Grandma moved in with us for a while. As a child of seven or eight, I started listening to the local radio station in Cape Girardeau with Grandma whenever the Cardinal baseball game came on. KMOX was, and still is, the flagship station, and we were so grateful to be entertained by our favorite team. You cannot imagine how I feel about those times I had at the radio with my grandma.[129]

Harvey Voss, an engineer at KMOX, retired in 1978 after nearly forty years at the station. He remembers one special broadcast in which he handled all the audio.

"This was the first time the St. Louis Symphony was ever broadcast in stereo. Arthur Fiedler was conducting from the Khorassan Room at the Chase Park-Plaza Hotel. There wasn't stereo radio as we know it today, but KMOX teamed up with KCFM. We ran two amplifiers, with KMOX taking the left track and KCFM taking the right track. To listen to the broadcast, you had to have both an AM radio and an FM radio on at the same time. It was an amazing feat — and it worked!"[130]

Bob Costas remembers some early advice he received from Bob Hardy.

"Bob came in at, I think 5:30 with Rex Davis, and the first thing I had to do was something on the FM station at 5:55 in the morning. Then I would go on with Bob and Rex to do the first sports report at 6:08. I've always hated to get up early in the morning, and my biggest weakness, my worst trait, is that I'm always late. I've gotten better at it, but I was never good at it. I would often come into the

Bob Hardy and Jim White fly a kite off the KMOX balcony during one of their Friday Happy Hour broadcasts. *Hardy Family Archives*

Jim Symington.

Chuck Percy.

John Danforth.

Lawrence K. Roos.

station late … and try to compose myself … and then come stumbling in to do the sports at 6:08 with Bob, who was the ultimate professional. A couple of times he laid down the law to me, but it was all from the standpoint of 'you can't do this to yourself, you can't be late.' He was nice and would say, 'You're too talented to go on the air less than 100 percent well prepared.'"[131]

Rich Dalton also got advice from Hardy when he was interning at KMOX.

"I was pretty green and unwise as to the ways of proper newsroom decorum. This means that I used to take my shoes and socks off while writing news for 'the man that walks and talks at midnight.' After all, it was three o'clock in the morning and nobody was there. I would deliver the news to him barefoot. He was so cool, that he didn't want to say right out that I was screwing up and that I should put my shoes on. One day I was called into Bob Hardy's office. He was the news director at the time. He said, 'Frank Stanton (president of CBS) has been known to walk in at 3 a.m. It wouldn't

Relaxing in the KMOX studios between shows in 1975. *Hardy Family Archives*

do to have one of the newswriters walking around in bare feet.' After that, I kept my shoes on!"[132]

One of Bob Costas' favorite stories about Mr. Hyland involves a Spirits basketball broadcast.

"I had been at KMOX for two months. I was supposed to do a Spirits game in Memphis. It's a Friday ... and I need my paycheck or I can't possibly embark on this road trip and have any kind of cash in my pocket. So I go upstairs to pick up my check, and they were closed for lunch. So I waited till they came back, got the check, ran across to Boatmen's, cashed the check, jumped in the car, and headed for the airport. But I had cut it too close, because with the traffic, I missed the plane. So the next plane is scheduled for six o'clock and the game starts at 8:05, but it's only about a 45-minute flight to Memphis, and if the plane is on time I can make it, and no one has to know. But it starts to rain and the plane is delayed and I literally don't get there until after the game had started. Well, this has never happened in the whole history of KMOX. On the road they didn't travel with a second broadcaster, so there was literally no broadcast. Bill Wilkerson was on the air telling the people there were technical difficulties, and as soon as those were cleared up, I would

Hardy and Rex Davis enjoying their morning.

be on the air. I came on with five minutes to go in the first quarter. Now, Mr. Hyland knew all about this, because he was on the phone to the guy at the airline, and getting reports from the cockpit and pulling all of his strings and everything. There were a lot of people, Bernie Fox included, who wanted me to be fired. Mr. Hyland had me come back to St. Louis (the trip was to go from Memphis to San Antonio), and I had to come back to St. Louis the following morning and face the music. I remember I sat down and he said, 'You know, I may be all alone on this. I'm the only one here who doesn't think you should be fired for this. But I definitely think you should be fired if it ever happens again. In fact, if anything like this ever happens again' — and this is like these weird things he would say — 'I'm going to cut your ears off.' I didn't want to turn into Vincent Van Gogh, so I had to make sure it never happened again. He said, 'But now it's all water over the dam, and we're forgetting about it.'"[133]

Anne Keefe's first experiences on "At Your Service" were a bit difficult.

"At first I had trouble because I was a New Yorker. I would ask questions but some people thought I was being pushy, so I called my mother who taught handi- capped children

Bob Costas.

in New York City, and she asked if it was my tone or what I was asking. I said, 'I don't know.' She said that when you teach, you feel your way through the first few days to see whether they're shy in the class or what, and then you suit your style to what you've got. And maybe the people in the Midwest are softer and more gentle, so maybe the trick is to ask the same questions but to ask it differently. So then I changed my style and that was the secret. I listened to how Bob [Hardy] did it. He could ask the hard questions but always with courtesy and sort of a friendliness. It was like 'I'm not baiting you, I'm just really curious and I'm sure the listeners are too.'"[134]

In a 1992 letter to Bob Hardy, Kathleen Mary Maloney wrote,

"I've been a KMOX listener for about fifty years, but recall coming home for lunch at noon when in grade school and Mom and Dad always had KMOX on the radio. You and Bill and Wendy get my

Wendy Wiese, Hardy and Jim White aboard the McDonald's Restaurant for a broadcast of the July Fourth festivities in 1986. *Hardy Family Archives*

day off to a good start."[135]

Bill Wilkerson recalls his first hockey broadcast.

"I'm working with Dan Kelly and we're doing football. On the way to a football game, Dan said, 'What do you think of hockey?' and I said, 'What do you mean, what do I think of hockey?' He said, 'Do you like it?' I said, 'It's a tremendous game.' He didn't say anything else…. Now we're in Philadelphia and it's halftime and the phone rings — it's Mr. Hyland and I'm wondering, 'What did we do?' Mr. Hyland said, 'Say, where's that hockey arena?' I said, 'Are you talking about the Philadelphia hockey arena?' He said, 'Yeah,' and I said, 'Well, it's right across the street, I'm looking at it right here.' He said, 'The Blues are playing there tonight, aren't they?' I said, 'Well, yes, after the football game, Dan's going over there.' He said, 'Go over there with him and do hockey,' and he hung up. I thought, 'Oh my God, he wants me to do hockey with Dan Kelly?' Dan thought it was hilarious. So we go over there, and I told Dan I couldn't do it. But he said he'd do the game, and I should just keep score and say something reasonably intelligent once in a while.

Mary Phelan, Hardy and Wendy Wiese on July 4, 1987. *Hardy Family Archives*

Unfortunately, at that time Philadelphia was very good and the Blues were very bad, and every time I started to write a score, Philadelphia scored again…. I had no idea who did what to whom or why."[136]

Kevin McCarthy, on the air for both KMOX and KLOU, remembers an election day.

"I worked a morning with Bob [Hardy] and it was an election day. This was right after the Berlin Wall had come down…. I thought it would behoove us to impress to people that perhaps they really should get out and vote on that particular day. And with that, I just rather bluntly said, 'Perhaps today is the day you should get off of your butts and go vote; then if you're not happy, you can carp about it.' The next day when I came into work, Mr. Hyland called me into the office and said, 'Kevin, yesterday you didn't tell people to get off their butts and vote, did you?' And I looked at him and I

Hyland, lower right, conducts a daily staff meeting. Around the table, counter clockwise from Hyland, Rich Gray, Bob Fulstone, Paul Grundhauser, Shirley Jacobi Bates, Mary Klein, Cathy Gamble, Bob Osborne, Judy Simms, Peggy Cohill, John Cooper and John Angelides. *Stankoven Media Services*

said, 'Yes sir, I did.' And there was a pause, and he said, 'Oh. Well, that's not us.'"[137]

Anne Keefe recalled in 1992, the one time she was called into Mr. Hyland's office.

"He said a listener had called, and he [Mr. Hyland] told me, 'Now it's not that I'm critical, but this is just unacceptable ... this person called and said that **you** said that you were a Democrat.... Seriously, I don't care what you are, but you must never say it on the air, and your broadcasting should **never** indicate what you are by what you say.'"[138]

Many people remember Miss Blue, including Bob Costas.

"Miss Blue was the cleaning lady, and she had been there for a long time. The way she told it, Jack [Carney] had her in the studio and started talking to her. She thought they were in a commercial, and she didn't know they were on the air. She had this natural personality and this natural kind of optimism, 'all is well' and 'everything will be fine.' He started talking to her and she started this homespun philosophy of hers, and it developed into where Jack would have people call up or write in for advice. Bill Wilkerson

Bob Hyland and Norma Wallner, his administrative assistant. *Stankoven Media Services*

recorded the opening thing with a kind of maudlin organ music and, 'Now again, it's time to hear from Miss Miriam Blue, who will counsel you about your troubles and tribulations.' And then she would come on and declare that all is well…. Someone would pose a question…. In many cases, she would give an inadvertently funny response and her bit of wisdom. Then I think she went on either "I've Got A Secret," or "To Tell The Truth," or "What's My Line?" as the cleaning lady who became the big radio star. I don't think she had ever been on a plane before, and certainly had never been to New York before. Everyone just loved her."[139]

Mrs. Florence Nellesen wrote with a fond memory.

I sent Bob Hardy and Rex Davis the recipe to my Sauerkraut Cake. On March 17, 1978, I received a note from Bob thanking me for the recipe.

'We tried it and it's pretty good. Can't seem to get the newsroom people to try it though. Maybe I shouldn't have told them what it was till *after* they tasted it. Thanks again, Rex and I both appreciate it. Happy Spring! Bob Hardy.'

I kept the note with my cake recipes all these years.[140]

Fortunately, the equipment

Dan Dierdorf and Hardy in 1978. *Hardy Family Archives*

has changed considerably over the years, as Harvey Voss recalls one of his toughest jobs,

*"One of the worst things I remember was at the old Sportsman's Stadium on Grand. It was a long way up to the broadcast booth and there was no elevator. We ran the amplifier off a large storage battery that was in a big box with handles, and it was **very** heavy carrying it up each week."*[141]

Rex Davis remembers early recorders,

"In the early 'At Your Service' years, I'd go out for a story and have to carry a fifty-pound recorder. Now they have recorders that fit in your pocket."[142]

Bob Costas remembers Bob Hyland's attempt at programming during the disco era.

"Mr. Hyland hired a guy named Otis 'Boogieman' Thomas around 1977 or something. He called me in his office, clearly because I was the youngest person on the staff, and said, 'What do you think of this disco trend?' And I said, 'Well, you know I'm not a big fan of it, but it is kind of big.' He said, 'There's a guy that sent me his tape,

Robert Hyland
Senior Vice President
CBS

1988 St. Louis MAN of the YEAR

1988 Man of the Year. *Rick Stankoven, January 1, 1989, St. Louis Post-Dispatch Magazine*

and I'm thinking of hiring him for FM and maybe using him on weekends when we don't have a sports event — Otis "Boogieman" Thomas, what do you know about him?' I told him I didn't really know the "Boogieman," but that disco was big and maybe he could give him a try. So he hires him, and two weeks later I get called into his office again. And on his desk are two or three letters from little old ladies, and he picks them up and says, 'Let me ask you something. Is there a song called, "I want to Kiss You All Over"?' I told him that I believed so…. And then he asked what a specific line from the song meant, and I said, 'Well Mr. Hyland, I could take a few guesses but I'm **sure** my first guess would be correct … and he went on and on that he didn't know there were songs like that, and that the "Boogieman" had to go!"[143]

Costas also recollects Hyland's tact.

"Hyland hired Scott St. James, who had been in St. Louis radio awhile. Scott had a great voice, was kind of a beach boy-looking type of guy, blond hair, tall … and he fancied himself as sort of a playboy. Scott comes on at 4:06 one day and says, 'Well, you know, if I seem just a little bit stunned, a little bit unlike myself today, I hope you'll understand why. Just seconds ago, a

Anne Keefe and Jeff Rainford in the newsroom. *KMOX*

giant bouquet of flowers was delivered to the studio; it's sitting right here on the desk with the following note — 'Cowboy, thanks for last night. Nobody does it better. Linda.' And then he goes on to explain, 'You know, my lady and I had been having sort of a tough time and I thought it's now or never. So I did a real first-class cabin number. I hired a limo, we went out to Tony's, and now this came. I guess things have worked out all right, and Linda, I dedicate this program to you. And now, here's Kathe Hartley.' At this point, people are coming out of their offices to watch him do this, and I'm almost under the table cracking up. So the next day, Mr. Hyland calls Scott into his office and he says, 'Scott do you like it here at KMOX, salary okay, staff okay, you enjoy it here?' Scott's saying, 'Oh, yes sir, great, everything is wonderful, it's like a dream come true.' Hyland says, 'Good, I'm glad everything is in order for you. Let me ask you one last thing. You haven't seen any cowboys around KMOX? You know ten-gallon hat, boots, spurs, chaps, anything like that?' Scott says, 'No, no I haven't Mr. Hyland.' And Hyland says, 'Well, if you do see any cowboys around here, you'll let me know won't you? Because if there's anything I can't stand, it's cowboys.

So you'll be the first to tell me if any cowboys are walking around KMOX won't you?' So that was how Mr. Hyland let him know that one more false move, and it would be all over."[144]

Bob Hyland visits with the morning crew, Bob Hardy, Wendy Wiese and Bill Wilkerson in the studio. *Stankoven Media Services*

I want to

share a few of my favorite memories of KMOX.

During the Gulf War, I lived in Dover, Delaware, with my husband who was in the Air Force, and our daughter, Stacey. Glen flew C-5s and was flying a lot, so we knew things were escalating but didn't know when the conflict would actually become a war. It was on January 16, 1991, and I was sitting in our car in front of Stacey's high school waiting for her to return from a swim meet. I wondered if I could pick up KMOX on the car radio (once in a while I heard Dad early in the morning), and I tried to tune 1120 in. I picked it up perfectly, and there, sitting in my car in Dover, I heard that we had gone to war.

Stacey was eleven years old, and had just come back from a week at Space Camp in Huntsville, Alabama. She was visiting her grandparents, and they were both impressed by the kinds of things that she had learned at Space Camp. Stacey spent hours telling them all about the space program, the booster rockets, the space capsules, everything. Dad decided to have her join him on the morning program, and he would interview her about going to Space Camp. He introduced her only as Stacey Chinn, and started asking questions. She answered everything in detail, and then he asked her to explain what the astronauts wear. She went into a detailed description of each of the seven or so different layers of the space suit, and the purpose of each layer. Everyone in the studio and control room was so impressed, and Dad had the biggest grin on his face — he was so proud of her. Then he said, 'Thank you, Stacey, for being here today.' And she said, 'Thank you, Grandpa!' And they cut to a commercial.

It was in the mid '60s, and John Davidson was probably at the height of his career. Dad was going to have him on the air, and I begged Dad to let me sit in the studio during the show. It was something we didn't do very often, and he finally agreed to it. I was a young teen-ager and had a huge crush on Davidson, so I spent hours getting ready to go to the station. I sat in the studio during the show but the best part was afterward, when Dad took my picture with John Davidson out on the balcony!

Bill Wilkerson sums it all up nicely.

"*The most endearing memory is of all the people to whom that station was more than a job. Bob Hardy would work sun-up to sundown if there was an election, or whatever, it didn't matter. It was just that something needed to be done, and he was going to do it. I was fortunate to come in when, and to know the people to whom, this job was a profession.*"[145]

Into the Future

In 1992 when Robert Hyland died, CBS had a decision to make — who would replace him and lead the station into the future. Rod Zimmerman, the vice president/general manager of WWJ/WJOI, the CBS stations in Detroit, was the company's pick to fill the vacant spot. Having listened to KMOX while growing up in Pekin, Illinois, as well as through his college days at Southern Illinois University at Carbondale, Zimmerman was the perfect choice. A graduate of the CBS School of Management, he would be the man at the helm as the station faced the day-to-day challenges of being the number one radio station in the St. Louis market.

There have been many changes at KMOX since Zimmerman took over — the sudden death of Bob Hardy, the retirement of Anne Keefe and John Angelides, the decision to air the "Rush Limbaugh Show," and the departure of several on-the-air personalities. However, through it all, Rod Zimmerman has kept his cool and kept KMOX on an even keel. Perhaps that's because he knows that through it all, KMOX's commitment to the community has not changed. The convictions and philosophies of those who gave so much to KMOX are still evident today.

As Zimmerman himself wrote,
KMOX is the premiere radio station of its kind in the country. On December 24, 1925, St. Louisans heard for the first time a radio

station that would become a part of their lives, as well as an integral part of this community. No one could have predicted the impact the station has made in the industry, the community and the everyday lives of its listeners.

Many have dedicated their careers to the benefit of the radio station. People like Robert Hyland, Jack Carney, Jack Buck and of course, Bob Hardy. They, along with many others who have worked at KMOX throughout the years, are the reason the radio station has grown to the stature it enjoys today. It's through our people, past and present, that we have been able to provide the kind of programming that has made KMOX number one for 30 years. Legendary broadcasters such as Harry Caray, Jim White, Bob Costas, Dan Dierdorf and countless others cut their teeth by going to the "KMOX University of Broadcasting."

We as a community enjoy this treasure because of those who built it. People like Bob Hardy who were on the cutting edge of their profession and who never thought twice about giving 150% to the success of the station. It is from this foundation that KMOX News/ Talk 1120 is positioned to move into the 21st Century. The commitment of the radio station has not changed since 1925. As "The Voice of St. Louis," KMOX is committed to quality programming, community service and supporting those who continue to make a difference ... as did Bob Hardy.

Rod Zimmerman
Vice President/General Manager, KMOX

Epilogue

KMOX, Bob Hardy and all of the voices of St. Louis have given us a legacy that is wide and wonderful. It encompasses all the voices that started their careers at KMOX and never knew how high they would climb; all the voices that have shared their expertise with students from around the country and helped them on their way, only to have them joyfully write back to let their mentors know where they were and what they were doing, not only in radio, but television as well; and not only voices, but technical "hands" as well, who have counseled over 2,000 stations from around the world on how to do it successfully.

KMOX opened a world of learning for us by opening our ears and minds to subjects we never thought about. It brought conversation to every dinner table and meeting, and made all of its listeners everywhere know what and who talk radio really was — a balanced, fair, and open forum.

It was a pleasure for me to be a part of all that, albeit from the sidelines. I will be forever grateful to all of you, from next door to around the world, who shared with me this wonderful opportunity of learning.

It was a joy for Bob to have found his niche in life. He had so much pride in and loyalty to "his" community and the station that allowed him to enter your households and become a part of each of your families.

Bob's love and dedication to his profession will carry on

through two scholarships established in his name at Southern Illinois University at Edwardsville. Each is a full two year scholarship for an entering junior studying Mass Communications. One of the requirements for consideration is an original essay on "Integrity in Broadcasting," an idea that defined Bob's career.

I am also happy to report that all of the material that was in Bob's archives: the audio tapes, scripts, articles and pictures, are being donated to the Missouri Historical Society in St. Louis.

Finally, my endearing love and thanks to our daughter, Sandy, for writing this book. Needless to say it probably was the challenge of her life, but oh so worthwhile.

Mrs. Bob (Rita) Hardy
1996

Appendices

Recipes

The philosophy of being a friend or a member of the family was shown by how much the listeners knew about the KMOX personalities, and the things they enjoyed when not on the air. For example, everyone knew about Hardy's farm called Wildflower and his bees, about White's boat, about Carney's travels and celebrity pals, about Wiese's pregnancies.

And just as family members and friends share recipes, so, too, did Bob Hardy and Jack Carney. Following are a few of their most requested recipes.

Pork Sausage
by Bob Hardy

Hi — thanks for asking for my pork sausage recipe. Hope it turns out as good for you as it did for me. This is for fifty pounds … if you're going to do it, might as well get some friends in to share the work — as well as the cost. It's more fun that way.

    50 lbs. of pork shoulder (boned and cut into strips)
    8 oz. butcher's salt
    4 oz. butcher's pepper (medium coarse grind)
    3/4 oz. nutmeg
    3 garlic cloves, quartered lengthwise, and covered with
    warm water, for one hour

Grind meat *one* time through medium cut grinder. Add salt, pepper, nutmeg and ONLY THE WATER from the garlic.

Now, here's where you make it or break it: hand mix the entire thing until the meat becomes stringy. You'll know when that occurs. Place in sausage stuffer and use natural casings if possible. That's it! (Naturally, you can halve the ingredients if necessary, but keep the proportions the same.)

I think you'll like it…. I know you'll enjoy making it.

Good luck!

Microwave Fudge

by Bob Hardy

1 lb. sifted confectioner's sugar
1/2 cup cocoa
1/4 cup milk
1/4 lb. butter or oleo

Combine in glass bowl, cook on high for 1 3/4 minutes. Remove from microwave oven, add 1 tablespoon vanilla, and stir with beaters till glossy (4 minutes). Pour into greased dish.

IT'S GREAT!!!

(The mixture will look almost the same when it comes *out* of the oven as it did when it went *in*. It won't melt down until you mix.)

Crock Pot Apple Butter
Bob Hardy

Cook quartered apples till soft. Put through sieve till you have 2 1/2 quarts of apples (sauce). Place in crock pot with:

2 1/2 cups sugar
3 sticks (or 1 tbsp) cinnamon
1/2 tsp. ground cloves

Cook on low for 24 to 36 hours (till thick). **Do not have lid on crock pot**. Can or freeze.

Spinach Salad

by Jack Carney

Thank you for writing for the Spinach Salad recipe. We find at home that we prepare this more than lettuce salad, making double dressing recipes and keeping at least a quart ready to go in the refrigerator. Good luck with the Spinach Salad. I think that you will find members of your family who dislike spinach will like this, so don't tell them.

2 bunches of spinach leaves torn like lettuce (remove large stems)
1 cup watercress (optional)
6 strips crisp bacon
2 hard boiled eggs

Dressing:
3/4 cup cider vinegar
1 cup oil
1/4 cup sugar
1 white onion, grated fine (use 1 tbsp. dehydrated onion if lazy)
1 tsp. dry mustard
1 tsp. salt
1 tsp. poppy seed
2 tsp. lemon juice

Place spinach leaves with stems removed in salad bowl and toss with dressing. Just before serving, crumble bacon and sprinkle over top the two chopped hard boiled eggs.

This makes a large amount of dressing, but it can be refrigerated.

Stand by for raves.

Southern Style Dressing
by Jack Carney

1 loaf stale white bread, pulled apart
1/2 stick oleo
5 medium onions, chopped
1/2 cups chopped celery
6 eggs, slightly beaten
1 cup chicken or turkey broth
1/2 tbsp. poultry seasoning

Melt butter. Sauté onions. Add celery and sauté. Take off heat and add salt, pepper and seasoning. Add bread, then eggs, then broth. Do not stir too much. Put in casserole and dot with butter. Bake uncovered at 350 degrees for 1/2 hour. Baste last half hour with turkey juice. Do not pack down in casserole.

Black Jack Barbecue Sauce

by Jack Carney

1 cup strong coffee
1 cup Worcestershire sauce
1 cup catsup
1/2 cup cider vinegar
1/2 cup brown sugar
3 tbsp. chili powder
3 tsp. salt
2 cups chopped onions
1/4 cup minced hot chili peppers
6 cloves garlic, minced

Combine all ingredients in a saucepan and simmer 25 minutes. Strain or puree in a blender or food processor. Refrigerate between uses.

Makes 5 cups.

Italian Slaw

by Jack Carney

1 medium head cabbage, shredded
1 medium onion, thinly chopped
7/8 cup sugar

Layer cabbage and onion in a bowl, top with sugar.

Dressing:
1 cup dark vinegar
3/4 cup salad oil
2 tsp. sugar
1 tsp. salt
1 tsp. dry mustard
1 tsp. celery seed

Bring mixture to a boil, while still hot, pour over cabbage.
Cover and let stand 4-6 hours. Mix and serve.

Can be stored in refrigerator 2-3 weeks.

Copper Pennies
by Jack Carney

2 lbs. carrots
1 green pepper
1 medium onion
1 can (10 1/2 oz.) tomato soup
1/2 cup oil
3/4 - 1 cup vinegar
2/3 - 3/4 cup sugar
1 tsp. worcestershire sauce
1 tsp. prepared mustard
1/2 tsp. salt

Slice, then cook carrots in salt water for 8-10 minutes, drain. Slice green peppers into thin strips. Slice onion thinly and separate into rings. Arrange carrots, green pepper and onions in dish.

For marinade: mix together tomato soup, oil, vinegar, sugar, Worcestershire sauce, mustard and salt. Pour marinade over vegetables in bowl.

Cover and leave in refrigerator several hours or overnight. Stir occasionally. This will keep about a week to 10 days in refrigerator.

April Fools'

The following is the script from April Fools' Day in 1977 when Hardy and Rex Davis decided to have some fun with the controversy over a proposed airport site in Illinois.

HARDY:

Following in the heels of the airport decision announced Tuesday, and the obvious disappointment of those favoring the Illinois site, Washington has decided to placate that disappointment by announcing a new project for Illinois — a fully-funded sea-plane port on the Kaskaskia River. A slough on the river will be dredged to a depth of nine feet, to conform with current environmental policy, and will be extended to 4,000 feet from its present 36 foot length. Rex Davis is on the site ... Rex?

DAVIS (muffled):

This is Rex Davis on the site of the newly proposed sea-plane port here near the Kaskaskia River. And following judicious investigative reporting techniques, we've uncovered a real problem. Part of the proposed extension of that river slough runs through a large patch of morel mushrooms, and here with me are representatives of MAD ... Mushroomers Against Dredging. They insist they'll keep the drag lines out of this area, no matter what Washington says. This is Rex Davis on the site.

HARDY:

Thank you, Rex. There's a parallel story here. Recreational

interests, torpedoed by the Meramec decision, see a new opportunity for boating, water skiing, and hydro-plane racing and are meeting at this moment in St. Genevieve. Rex Davis is there.

DAVIS (out of breath):

Whew! Fast trip. This is Rex Davis reporting from St. Genevieve where representatives of recreational interests, torpedoed by the Carter Meramec Decision, are regrouping. They see new possibilities for them in the newly proposed sea-plane site on the Kaskaskia River, but insist the 4,000-foot length and 100-foot width is in need of expansion. I'm told 100 feet won't allow enough room for the hydroplanes to turn around in. There's also a question of the 9-foot depth. These people want that to be at least 12 feet deep, and have commissioned a study to determine the feasibility. This is Rex Davis at St. Genevieve.

HARDY:

Thank you, Rex. Meanwhile, in Washington, the Illinois delegation is meeting with the U.S. Coast Guard, who has disputed jurisdiction over the Kaskaskia River site. A question of authority apparently exists between the Coast Guard and the Illinois River Patrol over who will control this new sea-plane site. Rex Davis is there in Washington ... Rex?

DAVIS:

This is Rex Davis in Washington. I've just left a meeting of the Illinois delegation, the Coast Guard and the State River patrol. And if you think things were fouled up before, listen to this! The FAA says *it* has authority over the proposed sea-plane site, and wants to build a ten million dollar control tower there to prove it. But while it admits the FAA has airspace control, the River patrol says once on the water, the planes are ours. And they want to build an eight million dollar floating lighthouse to prove it. The Coast Guard is so angry it's decided to pull all its recruiting offices out of Southern Illinois. This is Rex Davis in Washington.

HARDY:

This has just been handed to me. Members of the once-thought-to-be-defunct Save the Old Post Office Movement have issued plans to move the old post office from downtown St. Louis to the newly proposed sea-plane site on the Kaskaskia River, and turn it into a lodge. They need funds to do this, and are working on plans to get St. Louis school kids to donate pennies as they once did to buy the Santa Maria, pieces of which are still being dug up at the Kaskaskia site. Rex Davis is there.

DAVIS:

The Mushroomers Against Dredging are carefully studying some shells they've just overturned while picking morels here. One report is that they are much like the Higgins pearly mussel shell, but another fellow says they look more like standard 12-gauge. Meanwhile, surveyors are now on the scene, laying out the new route three bridges over the sea-plane port. Engineers from Missouri have been called in to plan that job. They are the same ones who designed the Vandeventer Overpass. This is Rex Davis holding the transit.

HARDY:

Word just in ... says a group of St. Louis County business-men are meeting at this hour to embark on an Illinois land-banking plan for a new, multi-team sports complex near the sea-plane site; one plan calls for a professional racquetball team to be known as the Indiana Bats. Rex Davis is there.

DAVIS:

This is Rex Davis in the county. These men say they have a complete package now, except for one small problem — a new lock and dam will have to be built near the proposed sports complex, to ensure the sea-plane site will not flood out any sports events. The lock and dam will be built near New Athens, but some residents there say they don't want it there. They want it closer to Scott Air Force Base. Scott officials here say send it to Richard Gebauer in Kansas City. And it goes on and on ... maybe another study — check with Senator Eagleton.

References

Biographical data of Bob Hardy from KMOX Radio

Clark AFRS AM & FM, Public Information Office, 13th Air Force, Clark Air Force Base, July 1953.

"Hardy: 'Lucky Guy,' " Greg Reeves, *Belleville News-Democrat*, January 30, 1976.

"Bob Hardy: KMOX Radio's Eye Opener," John Archibald, *St. Louis Post-Dispatch*, May 31, 1981.

"Interview with Condemned Man," *The Journal*, March 9, 1960.

"Blind kids 'see' circus," Edward J. Presberg, *St. Louis Globe-Democrat*, September 5, 1975.

Biographical data of Robert Hyland from KMOX Radio

KMOX Radio firsts-newscopy from KMOX

"KMOX-The Voice of St. Louis,"*Technician Engineer*, April 1963, p.4.

"From Lindbergh to Hyland: Fifty Years of St. Louis Radio," Alice English, December 24, 1975.

St. Louis Review, March 19, 1965.

"Profile of the New President of the Advertising Club of St. Louis," Ad Club Weekly, July 1962.

"The Man Behind the Voice of St. Louis," Ted Schafers, *St. Louis Globe-Democrat*, March 19-20, 1966.

"KMOX is 'At Your Service,'" Kathy Smith, 1972.

"Robert Hyland: Feared and Admired," John M. McGuire, *St. Louis Post-Dispatch*, May 14, 1979.

Robert F. Hyland Speech presented to Harvard Business School Club, September 9, 1980.

"1988 St. Louis Man of the Year," Mary Kimbrough, *St. Louis Post-Dispatch Magazine*, January 1, 1989.

"KMOX Head Hyland Dies of Cancer," *St. Louis Post-Dispatch*, March 6, 1992.

"Remembering Robert Hyland," John M. McGuire, *St. Louis Post-Dispatch*, March 8, 1992.

St. Louis Post-Dispatch, March 3, 1996.

St. Louis Daily Globe-Democrat: 12/11/25, 12/19/25, 12/20/25, 12/25/25, 1/4/26, 1/17/26, 3/24/26, 4/30/26, 7/31/26, 12/5/26, 12/19/26, 7/18/27, 10/2/27, 4/21/28, 6/13/28, 5/17/29, 1/19/30, 5/29/30, 12/22/30, 2/2/31, 3/1/31, 6/21/31, 5/27/32, 6/17/33, 7/16/33, 9/12/38, 3/22/46, 3/26/47, 4/9/47, 2/14/49, 2/17/55, 11/28/55, 1/6/57, 2/27/57, 4/20/57, 11/17/57, 4/1/58, 4/15/58, 5/4/58, 10/17/58, 8/31/59, 10/20/59, 2/18/60, 5/6/60, 5/19/60

"Lady in the Dark," *St. Louis Globe-Democrat Magazine*, March 31, 1957.

"Founder of 'Hot Stove League' Helped KMOX to Become the 'Sports' Voice of America, Brian C. Hauswirth, *The Reporter*, September 19, 1989.

"KMOX and Baseball," Eric Mink, *St. Louis Post-Dispatch*, July 9, 1981.

"What convicts think is voiced over St. Louis radio station," *Menard Times*, December 1, 1965.

"Information for Guests" letter, KMOX Radio archives, 1969.

"KMOX Radio-The Voice of St. Louis," KMOX Radio archives, 1973.

"Radio Reviews," *Variety*, March 16, 1960.

1957 KMOX Annual Report

KMOX Chronology and Historical Data

CBS Annual Shareholders Meeting Statistics, April 1978.

KMOX Memorandum, RE:Another KMOX Radio First, Aline Surmeyer, August 12, 1976.

"It's all talk, talk, talk," Peter Hernon, *St. Louis Globe-Democrat*, March 23, 1979.

"KMOX Radio personality has hardy ratings Down Under,"
    Pete Rahn, *St. Louis Globe-Democrat*, September 14, 1983.
KMOX taped transcripts, Robert Hyland tribute, March 6-7,
    1992.
KMOX taped transcripts, Bob Hardy tribute, April 18-19, 1993.
Hardy Family Archives
Hyland Family Archives

Personal Interviews
Jim Butler, December 1994
John Sabin, April 1995
Bob Costas, July 1995
Rex Davis, July 1995
John Angelides, August 1995
Jack Buck, November 1995
Bill Wilkerson, January 1996
Kevin McCarthy, February 1996
Jeanette Hoag Grider, June 1996
Jim White, August 1996

Telephone Interviews
Anne Keefe, August 1996
Harvey Voss, August 1996
Randy Karraker, August 1996
Charles Brennan, September 1996

Written Communications
Rich Dalton, April 1996
Mary Anne Hagedorn, August 1995
Jill Grimes, September 1995
Carol Reigle, September 1995
Florence Nellesen, August 1995
David Christoff (to Bob Hardy), March 1992
Kathleen Mary Maloney (to Bob Hardy), March 1992
Lt. Stephen Knight (to Bob Hardy), December 1990

Endnotes

1. Bob Costas interview, July 1995.
2. Hardy Family archives, taped transcripts of Bob Hardy tribute broadcast on KMOX Radio, April 18-19, 1993.
3. Ibid.
4. Ibid.
5. Ibid.
6. Ibid.
7. *St. Louis Daily Globe-Democrat*, December 25, 1925.
8. *St. Louis Daily Globe-Democrat*, December 19, 1925.
9. *St. Louis Daily Globe-Democrat*, December 11, 1925.
10. op.cit. 8.
11. op.cit. 7.
12. op.cit. 7.
13. op.cit. 7.
14. *St. Louis Daily Globe-Democrat*, January 17, 1926.
15. *St. Louis Daily Globe-Democrat*, January 4, 1926.
16. *St. Louis Daily Globe-Democrat*, December 20, 1925.
17. *St. Louis Daily Globe-Democrat*, March 24, 1926.
18. *St. Louis Daily Globe-Democrat*, February 2, 1931.
19. Harvey Voss interview, August 1996.
20. *St. Louis Daily Globe-Democrat*, February 14, 1949.
21. "1988 St. Louis Man of the Year," Mary Kimbrough, *St. Louis Post-Dispatch Magazine*, January 1, 1989.
22. "Profile of the New President of the Advertising Club of St. Louis," Ad Club Weekly, July 1962.

23. Robert Hyland Biographical data from KMOX Radio.
24. "The Man Behind the Voice of St. Louis," by Ted Schafers, *St. Louis Globe-Democrat*, March 19-20, 1966.
25. Hyland Family archives, taped transcripts from Robert Hyland Tribute broadcast on KMOX Radio, March 6-7, 1992.
26. *St. Louis Post-Dispatch*, March 3, 1996.
27. op.cit. 25.
28. Rich Dalton letter, April 1996.
29. op.cit. 25.
30. op.cit. 25.
31. op.cit. 28.
32. op.cit. 25.
33. op.cit. 25.
34. op.cit. 25.
35. op.cit. 25.
36. "Robert Hyland: Feared and Admired," John M. McGuire, *St. Louis Post-Dispatch*, May 14, 1979.
37. Robert F. Hyland speech presented to Harvard Business School Club, September 9, 1980.
38. op.cit. 25.
39. op.cit. 25.
40. "Bob Hardy: KMOX Radio's Eye Opener," John Archibald, *St. Louis Post-Dispatch*, May 31, 1981.
41. Jim Butler interview, December 1994.
42. "Clark AFRS AM & FM," Public Information Office, 13th Air Force, Clark Air Force Base, July 1953.
43. op.cit. 25.
44. op.cit. 25.
45. "It's all talk, talk, talk," Peter Hernon, *St. Louis Globe-Democrat*, March 23, 1979.
46. op.cit. 41.
47. Bob Hardy Eulogy statement by Charles Brennan, given at St. Louis Marconi Awards, May 1993.
48. op.cit. 2.
49. op.cit. 2.
50. op.cit. 2.
51. op.cit. 2.

52. op.cit. 1.
53. "Blind kids 'see' circus," Edward J. Presberg, *St. Louis Globe-Democrat*, September 5, 1975.
54. "From Lindbergh to Hyland: Fifty Years of St. Louis Radio," Alice English, December 24, 1975.
55. op.cit. 41.
56. 1957 KMOX Annual Report, p.16.
57. Ibid., page 7-8.
58. KMOX Historical Data
59. *St. Louis Daily Globe-Democrat*, October 17, 1958.
60. *St. Louis Daily Globe-Democrat*, August 31, 1959.
61. "KMOX is 'At Your Service,'" Kathy Smith, 1972.
62. Hyland Family archives, recording of daily staff meeting, February 16, 1960.
63. Ibid.
64. Ibid.
65. Pete Rahn column, *St. Louis Globe-Democrat*, February 18, 1960.
66. op.cit. 40.
67. Hyland Family archives, from KMOX broadcast, February 29, 1960.
68. Pete Rahn column, *St. Louis Globe-Democrat*, May 19, 1960.
69. Ibid.
70. "Radio Reviews," *Variety*, Wednesday, March 16, 1960.
71. John Sabin interview, April 1995.
72. op.cit. 25.
73. op.cit. 41.
74. op.cit. 25.
75. op.cit. 25.
76. op.cit. 41.
77. Jack Buck interview, November 15, 1995.
78. KMOX archives, Information for Guests letter, 1969 (or after).
79. op.cit. 25.
80. KMOX archives, "KMOX Radio-The Voice of St. Louis," 1973.

81. Hardy Family archives.

82. op.cit. 25.

83. Rex Davis interview, July 1995.

84. op.cit. 2.

85. op.cit. 1.

86. op.cit. 1.

87. op.cit. 25.

88. Kevin McCarthy interview, February 1996.

89. Jeanette Hoag Grider interview, June 1996.

90. op.cit. 25.

91. Hardy Family archives, letter to Bob Hardy from Lt. Stephen Knight, 726th Tactical Control System, U.S. Air Force, December 1990.

92. op.cit. 1.

93. op.cit. 77.

94. op.cit. 1.

95. op.cit. 41.

96. op.cit. 28.

97. Jim White interview, August 1996.

98. op.cit. 28.

99. op.cit. 97.

100. op.cit. 97.

101. op.cit. 97.

102. op.cit. 97.

103. op.cit. 97.

104. op.cit. 25.

105. op.cit. 25.

106. op.cit. 1.

107. op.cit. 77.

108. op.cit. 77.

109. op.cit. 88.

110. John Angelides interview, August 1995.

111. op.cit. 97.

112. op.cit. 97.

113. op.cit. 2.

114. op.cit. 25.

115. op.cit. 25.

116.op.cit. 25.

117. Charles Brennan interview, September 1996.

118. Mary Anne Hagedorn letter, August 1995.

119. op.cit. 2.

120. op.cit. 89.

121. op.cit. 89.

122. op.cit. 89.

123. Jill Grimes letter, September 1995.

124. op.cit. 2.

125. op.cit. 2.

126. Carol Reigle letter, September 1995.

127. Bill Wilkerson interview, January 1996.

128. Ibid.

129. Hardy Family archives, David Christoff letter, March 1992.

130. op.cit. 19.

131. op.cit. 1.

132. op.cit. 28.

133. op.cit. 1.

134. Anne Keefe interview, August 1996.

135. Hardy Family archives, Kathleen Mary Maloney letter, March 1992.

136. op.cit. 25

137. op.cit. 25.

138. op.cit. 25.

139. op.cit. 1.

140. Florence Nellesen letter, August 1995.

141. op.cit. 19.

142. op.cit. 83.

143. op.cit. 1.

144. op.cit. 1.

145. op.cit. 127.

Index

Fox, Bernie   147

G

H

I

J

K

L

London   30

M

Mack, Bill   30
Magsaysay, President Ramon   52
Malone, Ted   81
Maloney, Kathleen Mary   148
Mangner, Ted   69
Marciano, Rocky   52
Mart Building   34, 37, 68
Mathews, Ed   52
Mayfair Hotel   18, 21, 24, 35
Mayor's Town Meetings, The   95
Mays, Willie   123
McCarthy, J. Roy   80
McCarthy, Kevin   109, 111, 113, 119, 134, 150
McCormick, John   81, 128-129, 141
McDonnell Douglas   59
McGovern, George   103-105
McKendree College   63
Mead, Margaret   85
Menard Prison   95
Merchants Exchange   18, 23
Merton, Chester   24
Mexico   22, 80, 127
Miami Beach   103
Military Airlift Command   119
Miller, Don   102
Miss Blue   151
Miss Nanette   81
Mississippi Valley Trust Company   17-18
Missouri Broadcasters   63
Missouri School for the Blind   63
Mitchell, Don   91
Money   58
Moscow Radio   58, 110, 117
Municipal Opera   37

N

Narcotics Service Council   91
National Conference of Christians and Jews   38
National Football League   125
National Headliner Award   59, 105, 118
National Safety Council   70
Nellesen, Florence   152
Netherlands   80

New Zealand 22
Newman, Doug 129
Newsweek 57
Nixon, Richard 52

O

Officer Candidate School 53
Old Cathedral 42
Operation Weather Alert 69
Osborne, Bob 140

P

Paley, William 41
Pappy Cheshire 37
Payne, Lou 127
Peabody Award 63, 93
Persian Gulf War 59, 118
Philippine Islands 50
Prague 113, 114
Pun of the Day 99

R

Radio Bridge 58, 110, 117
Radio Training School 34
Rahn, Pete 78
Reagan, Ronald 85
Red Square 112-113, 117
Reigle, Carol 141
RIAS 114
Rice, Jerry 123
Rodemich, Gene 24
Roosevelt, Eleanor 85
Rowan, Steve 81
Royal Canadian Mounted Police 36

S

Sabin, John 80
St. James, Scott 154
St. Louis Blues 125, 149
St. Louis Board of Education 70
St. Louis Browns 30, 39
St. Louis Cardinals 39, 72, 123, 124, 125
St. Louis Globe-Democrat 18, 22, 23, 24, 28, 38, 70, 81
St. Louis Hawks 81, 125
St. Louis Heart Association 63

USO   63
Utt, Arthur   23

V

Variety   78
Voss, Harvey   37, 141, 153

W

Wagner Electric Co.   18, 24
Wall Street Journal, The   41, 78
Wallace, Ada   30
Wallace, George   85
Warnick, Jack   129
Warsaw   113, 117
Washington University   66
Washington Week   106
WBBM   20, 33, 40
Weber, Dr. Alfred   81
WEW   39
White, Bill   126
White, Jim   57, 127, 129-132, 134-136
WIBV   53
Widmann, Nancy   41
Wiese, Wendy   43, 82, 139
WIL   53-55, 107
Wilke, Eugene   41
Wilkerson, Bill   82, 125, 141, 146, 149-150, 151-152, 157
World Series   27
WTAD   40

Y

Young, Kevin   113
Youth in the Shadows   69

Z

Zeleranskaya, Tatiana   117
Zumwalt, Admiral Elmo   58